D1453843

IN
SHEEP'S
CLOTHING

IN SHEEP'S CLOTHING

Jude's Urgent Warning about
Apostasy in the Church

O. S. HAWKINS

LOIZEAUX
Neptune, New Jersey

Unless otherwise indicated, Scripture taken from the
HOLY BIBLE: NEW INTERNATIONAL VERSION ®. NIVR.
Copyright © 1973, 1978, 1984 by International Bible Society.
Used by permission of Zondervan Publishing House
and Hodder & Stoughton Ltd.

The "NIV" and "New International Version" trademarks are
registered in the United States Patent and Trademark Office by
International Bible Society.

Library of Congress Cataloging-in-Publication Data
Hawkins, O. S.
In sheep's clothing: Jude's urgent warning about apostasy in the
church / O. S. Hawkins.
Includes bibliographical references.
ISBN 0-87213-325-7 (cloth)
1. Bible. N.T. Jude—Criticism, interpretation, etc.
2. Apostasy—Biblical teaching. I. Title.
BS2815.6.A66H38   1994
227'.9706—dc20   94-22540 CIP

Printed in the United States of America
10 9 8 7 6 5 4 3 2 1

TABLE OF CONTENTS

Introduction 9

Chapter One: Apostasy Viewed Theoretically 13

Chapter Two: Apostasy Viewed Apologetically 21

Chapter Three: Apostasy Viewed Synthetically 31

Chapter Four: Apostasy Viewed Apathetically 41

Chapter Five: Apostasy Viewed Prophetically 51

Chapter Six: Apostasy Viewed Cosmetically 73

Chapter Seven: Apostasy Viewed Sympathetically 93

Chapter Eight: Apostasy Viewed Pragmatically 113

Notes 123

Introduction

Eli Cohen, the son of a Jewish tie maker, was born in 1924 in the Jewish quarter of Alexandria, Egypt, and grew up speaking fluent Arabic. Every Israeli and anyone knowledgeable of Israel's history during the last forty years knows his name. In 1961 he was sent to Damascus, Syria, by the Mossad (the Israeli Intelligence Agency) to pose as a wealthy Arab businessman who had holdings in Buenos Aires. He quickly engaged himself in the import-export business and secured an apartment in the wealthiest area of Damascus. Not long afterward, he began giving large sums of money to Syrian politicians and quickly moved into the high social circles of Damascus. He was a regular guest at parties in the presidential palace and became a personal confidant of many governmental leaders. It was not unusual for him to be invited to high-level briefings at the Syrian-Israeli border.

At that time, Israel was dependent on pipelines in Galilee for its water supply. Those pipelines were vulnerable to attack from the Golan Heights, which was under Syrian control. Through his political connections, Eli learned that the Syrians were moving ahead with a plan to cut off Israel's water supply. While visiting the Syrian frontier, Eli convinced President Al-Hafez to plant eucalyptus trees surrounding the major military installations on the Golan Heights. These, Eli promised, would provide good cover and shield the installations from air surveillance.

Cohen's life of espionage was uncovered in 1965, and he was hanged in the town square of Damascus. A few months later, during the famous Six Day War, Israeli fighter pilots had little trouble knocking out all the Syrian military installations on the Golan Heights because of the information Eli had supplied. The pilots simply looked for patches of eucalyptus trees! Today the Golan Heights is in Israeli control because an impostor by the name of Eli Cohen provided valuable intelligence information while posing as a wealthy Arab businessman.

An impostor who infiltrates an organization can be a very dangerous threat. This is the warning found near the end of the

New Testament in the Epistle of Jude. In Jude's words, "certain men whose condemnation was written about long ago have secretly slipped in among you. They are godless men, who change the grace of our God into a license for immorality and deny Jesus Christ our only sovereign and Lord"(4). These impostors are also at work today in the church, Christian schools, and seminaries. Like Eli Cohen, they have crept in unnoticed and seek to destroy the work of God from within.

During the early days of the church, believers met tremendous opposition. Satan tried to destroy the church from without by means of persecution. Those of us who know church history know that through the centuries the blood of the martyrs has been the seed of church growth. The more the church has been persecuted, the more it has flourished. In our generation, we have seen this happen with the church in China.

Today however Satan is using strategies other than external persecution. It almost seems that during these last days Satan has said, "All right, if I can't destroy the church from without, I will seek to do so from within. I'll destroy the foundation of the Word of God, the faith on which the church is built."

Persecution from without does not destroy the church. Persecution simply makes it stronger. Apostasy from within takes the life and heart away from the church. Many denominations can attest to this truth today. Once they were thriving, vibrant, and alive, but now they are dead or dying. What happened? The damage certainly didn't happen from without. It happened from within! Apostates who have turned from God's truth have "secretly slipped in" and are destroying spiritual foundations of the church from within.

One of the most obvious platforms for apostasy has emerged in the field of education. Institutions of higher learning such as Harvard, Yale, Brown, Dartmouth, and Princeton have much in common. Yes, they are all universities. Yes, they are all in the Ivy League. Yes, they have existed for scores and scores of years. But many of us have forgotten that they were all founded for the express purpose of propagating the gospel of the Lord Jesus Christ. Their primary reason for being established was to bring glory to God. Tragically, somewhere along the way they left their high calling.

Three thousand years ago, King David asked this probing question: "When the foundations are being destroyed, what can the righteous do?"(Psalm 11:3) In this day and age, many of our ethical and ecclesiastical foundations are crumbling before our eyes. There is a great apostasy in our midst. Some denominations, schools, and churches that once held the Bible in high regard seem now to have little respect for it. Is it any wonder then that Jude admonished, "Dear friends, although I was very eager to write to you about the salvation we share, I felt I had to write to urge you to contend for the faith that was once for all entrusted to the saints"(3). If our generation fails to contend for this faith that has been delivered to us, we will be held accountable when the spiritual foundations are destroyed.

The Epistle of Jude deals with apostasy. Simply defined, apostasy is a turning away from the truth. Maxwell Coder, defines an apostate as "one who has received light but not life." Apostates claim to be Christians, but they are not. Nor are they merely unbelievers. Apostates know the truth but do not act upon it. They perform an inside job and are tools of the enemy to destroy the foundation of the church even though they themselves may be blind to this reality. The apostate may have received the written Word in some way but not the living Word—the Lord Jesus Christ.

Judas is a perfect example of an apostate. He had light but not life. He claimed to be a believer. For three and a half years he had nearly perfect attendance with our Lord Jesus and His band of disciples. In fact, he served as treasurer of that entourage. But he fell away! Later Jesus revealed that He knew from the beginning that Judas was not an authentic apostle. Since even Jesus' band of disciples had an apostate, we should not be surprised that apostates have infiltrated churches and denominations today. The book of Jude was written to expose them and to exhort us to "contend for the faith" (3).

Jude was careful in his warnings of apostasy to emphasize that an apostate has never been genuinely saved. Although the apostate knows the truth, he or she never acted upon it. As a result, one who studies the Epistle of Jude may be prone to ask, "Can I lose my salvation?" Realizing that this question will arise, Jude wanted true believers to know that they are kept by Jesus Christ.

In order that true believers might know that they are eternally secure, Jude began and ended the book with some of the greatest words of assurance ever written for the believer. In the first verse he wrote to those "who have been called, who are loved by God the

Father and kept by Jesus Christ." He then concluded the book by reminding us that the Lord "is able to keep you from falling, and to present you before His glorious presence without fault with great joy"(24). Clearly, apostates are unsaved. They have not lost their salvation; they never had it. One who is truly saved, however, is kept by Jesus Christ forever.

Why is it important for the church to study the book of Jude today? Just as the book of Acts describes the beginning of the church age, Jude describes the end of the church age. Since Acts has been referred to as the Acts of the Apostles, someone has suggested that Jude could well be named the Acts of the Apostates. Paul joins Jude in reminding us that "In later times some will abandon the faith"(1 Timothy 4:1). The book of Jude joins hands with other New Testament Epistles to sound the alarm and wake the church out of its slumber so that it might "contend for the faith that was once for all entrusted to the saints."

Eli Cohen sneaked into a foreign country under an impostor's guise and set out to destroy that country's foundations. However, his work was not nearly as damaging as that of Satan's secret agents today who have infiltrated churches, schools, and denominations, seeking to destroy their spiritual foundations by casting doubt on the authority and infallibility of the Word of God. As Jude wrote, they have "secretly slipped in." Before writing anything else, Jude urged the believer who is called and kept to earnestly contend for the faith—the Word of God.

Our Lord Jesus addressed the issue of apostasy warning us to "watch out for false prophets. They come to you in sheep's clothing, but inwardly they are ferocious wolves" (Matthew 7:15). Since the Lord Himself had a man "in sheep's clothing" among his inner group of disciples should we be surprised that such impostors are in our churches and schools today? They use our terminology and orthodox vocabulary but with completely different meanings. Jude's letter has never been more relevant than in our generation and serves to warn today's church of those among us who are IN SHEEP'S CLOTHING.

CHAPTER ONE
Apostasy Viewed Theoretically

Jude, a servant of Jesus Christ and a brother of James, To those who have been called, who are loved by God the Father and kept by Jesus Christ: Mercy, peace and love be yours in abundance (Jude 1-2).

I. WHO WE ARE IN CHRIST
II. WHAT WE HAVE IN CHRIST

T he *World Book Dictionary* defines the word *theoretical* in the following way: "planned or worked out in the mind; not from experience, not from fact." So it is accurate to say that the apostate claims, theoretically, to be a Christian. He professes the Lord Jesus with his lips but does not possess Him with his life. To the apostate, Christianity is theoretical, not experiential.

In dealing with apostasy in a theoretical sense, Jude wanted us to know who we are in Christ so that we might recognize apostasy. Therefore, he began with sweet words of assurance that remind us of who we are and what we have in Christ. Once we see who we as true believers really are and what we have, we can contrast the sincere saint with the synthetic saint, who is the apostate.

In the opening verse of Jude's Epistle he briefly revealed his identity both in terms of a heavenly relationship and an earthly relationship. Although Jude could have identified himself as the half brother of the Lord Jesus, for they shared the same earthly mother, he identified himself first in terms of a heavenly relationship. He told us much by calling himself "a servant of Jesus Christ." The Greek word used in this verse is *doulos* which can be translated "slave" or "bondservant." Jude was saying that he is one who wears the chains of love, one who has found his liberty in becoming a slave to Christ. A person becomes a bond-servant by purchase. Jude was mindful that his life was not his own and that it had been bought with a price.

Next, Jude went on to identify himself not only in terms of a heavenly relationship but in terms of an earthly relationship. He referred to himself as a "brother of James." James was the head of the Jerusalem church and the other half brother of our Lord. Maxwell Coder astutely observed that James wrote his Epistle to inform us of the importance of good works and that Jude wrote his Epistle to inform us of the danger of evil works.[1]

I. WHO WE ARE IN CHRIST

In Jude 1, we see the blessed Trinity at work. Authentic believers are called by the Spirit, beloved by the Father, and kept by the Lord Jesus Christ. Jude said that we are "called," which means we have received "an official summons." As true believers, we have been summoned by God. Salvation does not begin with us. If it did, we could lose it. Salvation begins with God, who began the good work in us and continues it. He takes the initiative. Peter reminded us too, that we "are a chosen people, a royal priesthood, a holy nation, a people belonging to God, that you may declare the praises of him who called you out of darkness into his wonderful light" (1 Peter 2:9).

I remember the day I was called. I had heard the outward call of the Gospel many times, but the day I heard the inward call was different. Just as Lazarus came forth out of the grave when he heard the Lord Jesus call his name, so I, as a seventeen-year-old, came out of spiritual death into spiritual life at the call of the Lord Jesus Christ. Like Lydia in the book of Acts, whose heart the Lord "opened" (Acts 16:14), God called me out of spiritual darkness into His marvelous light. Likewise, every true believer has been called from spiritual death unto spiritual life, from darkness into light.

In this first verse of Jude, it is as if he is saying, "Look at who we are! We are the called of God! We are a chosen people, a royal priesthood, called of God!"

Jude went on to say that we are not only "called of God" but are "loved by God the Father." Many translations use the word "beloved."[2] Those who are beloved are set apart for God Himself. He has called us and brought us out of the world, washed us in His blood, and set us apart for Himself.

Love has a way of setting one's beloved apart. When a man loves a woman and marries her, for example, he sets her apart from all others for his very own. I may love you, but my wife, Susie, is my beloved! There is quite a difference between those who are loved and the beloved. God loves the spiritually lost, but those who are saved are his beloved.

It's a wonderful thing to know that we are the beloved of God the Father. Jesus alluded to this in His high intercessory prayer. Hear Him on the evening before the crucifixion as He prayed to the Father:

> My prayer is not for them alone. I pray also for those who will believe in me through their message, that all of them may be one, Father, just as you are in me and I am in you. May they also be in us so that the world may believe that you have sent me. I have given them the glory that you gave me, that they may be one as we are one: I in them and you in me. May they be brought to complete unity to let the world know that you sent me and have loved them even as you have loved me (John 17:20-23).

Oh, to think that we are beloved of God the Father. The apostle John expressed it this way: "How great is the love the Father has lavished on us, that we should be called children of God!" (1 John 3:1a) We are so precious to God the Father. When I look at these words in Jude 1, which remind me that I am beloved of the Father, I think about how much I love my children. The overwhelming truth is that our heavenly Father loves us even more than we love our children. Our Father's love is beyond compare.

There is nothing we can do to make God love us more than He loves us right now. There is nothing we can do to make Him love us any less, either. He does not love us because we are valuable or worthy: we are valuable and worthy because He loves us. The Bible says that nothing can separate us from this love (Romans 8:38-39).

Are you beginning to see who we really are as true believers? God calls us out of spiritual darkness into His marvelous light. We are beloved by God the Father, but that is not all! Jude goes on to remind us that we are "kept by Jesus Christ." The word translated "kept," *tereo,* means "to watch; to guard over."[3] In its original language, this word is in the perfect tense, which indicates past completed action that has continuing results. It could best be translated, "continually kept."[4] When we stumble spiritually, for example, God keeps us from falling. We are kept by the Lord Jesus Christ!

I remember when our little daughter began to walk. She would reach up with chubby little fingers, grab my index finger, and hang on with all her might. She would then take a step or two, let go, and fall to the ground. It did not take too long before I learned an important lesson. I would reach down, take hold of her hand, and when she stumbled I would be there to hold her up and teach her to walk.

What a perfect analogy this is of the way in which our heavenly Father assists us. Our salvation is not dependent on our holding on to the bitter end. God reaches down and grabs hold of us. When we stumble spiritually, He is always there to help us along.

It is important for believers to realize that we are no safer than the One who keeps us. The good news is we do not keep our own salvation, God keeps us! Paul wrote, "That is why I am suffering as I am. Yet I am not ashamed, because I know whom I have believed, and am convinced that he is able to guard what I have entrusted to him for that day" (2 Timothy 1:12). In a similar way, Jude cautiously reminded true believers that they are kept safe by Christ Jesus for all eternity. Apostates, on the other hand, sin and fall and suffer condemnation.

We should remember that an apostate is not a true believer who walks away from his salvation. That is impossible, according to Scripture. An apostate professes but does not possess. Peter made it clear that apostates are not God's sheep. Instead they are like pigs and dogs. This point is clearly expressed in 2 Peter 2:21-22:

> It would have been better for them not to have known the way of righteousness, than to have known it and then to turn their backs on the sacred command that was passed on to them. Of them the proverbs are true: "A dog returns to its vomit," and, "a sow that is washed goes back to her wallowing in the mud."

We might clean up a pig on the outside, take it to the county fair, and show it off but that will not change its nature. The pig will go right back to the mire and slop of the pigpen as soon as it has a chance.

When I remember that I am kept by Christ and kept for Him as His bride, what right do I have to seek the things of this world instead of Him? What right do I have to put anything or anyone before Him? The writer of Hebrews gives us a clue as to how we are kept by and for Christ. He wrote, "Therefore he [Christ] is able to save completely those who come to God through him, because he always lives to intercede for them" (Hebrews 7:25).[5] How does Christ keep us? He prays for us. He asked God to keep us when, the evening before the crucifixion, he prayed, "I will remain in the world no longer, but they are still in the world, and I am coming to you. Holy Father, protect them by the power of your name—the name you gave me—so that they may be one as we are one" (John 17:11).

As we'll see later in more detail, Jude summed up his Epistle by writing, "To him who is able to keep you from falling and to present you before his glorious presence without fault and with great joy" (24). He wanted us all to make sure that we know who keeps us from falling. It is not we, it is He!

I would do anything I could to keep one of my children from falling and being hurt, and I am only human. How much more does God the Father keep us from falling. Jude wanted us to remember that we are called, beloved, and kept by the Lord. In contrasting the counterfeit Christian with the committed Christian, Jude went on to reveal not just who we are in Christ but what we have in Christ.

II. WHAT WE HAVE IN CHRIST

Jude informed us that as true believers we are the recipients of three important graces of God: mercy, peace, and love. And he requested that the Father would bestow these gifts "in abundance," knowing that only with such grace can the church cope with apostasy during these last days. The graces of our God— mercy, peace, love—defeat the apostate enemy. The shortest way for sinners to see their need of salvation is to let them see the sanctification of saints!

I believe Jude revealed in verse 2 what many of us have forgotten.

That is, there are only three basic relationships in life: our relationship with God, our relationship with ourselves, and our relationship with others. Jude began to show us not only who we are, but what we have as a result of these three relationships.

Our Relationship with God

In our relationship with God, we are recipients of God's mercy. This is what I call the "upward expression" because we receive mercy from above. During days of apostasy, we especially need God's mercy. That is why the Word exhorts us to "approach the throne of grace with confidence so that we might receive mercy and find grace to help us in our time of need" (Hebrews 4:16). God, in His mercy, does not give us what we deserve. Aren't we thankful that He has mercy on us and that morning by morning new mercies we see! The Bible says that God is "rich in mercy," and His mercy continues to forgive our sin.

Who are we? We are called by God out of spiritual darkness into His marvelous light. We are beloved of the Father. We are kept by the Lord Jesus Christ. What do we receive as believers? Through our relationship with God, we receive mercy.

Our Relationship with Ourselves

We also experience a relationship with ourselves. This is what I call the "inward expression" of peace. If we receive mercy from God, we obtain peace within our hearts. Thus, Jude pronounced upon believers the blessing of peace.

Many people who search, grope, and struggle for inner peace never find it because peace—the inward expression—only comes after the upward expression of God's mercy is received. This peace about which Jude wrote comes from God. It is His peace, not ours. Jesus said, "Peace I leave with you: my peace I give you; I do not give to you as the world gives. Do not let your hearts be troubled and do not be afraid" (John 14:27).

The only way we can be at peace within ourselves is to be at peace with God, but the upward expression of God's mercy must precede the inward expression of our peace. Do you have God's peace that Jude prayed would be yours in abundance? If not, it is because you have not received God's mercy.

Our Relationship with Others

Finally, Jude referred in verse 2 to our relationship with others. This is the "outward expression" of love. Once we have received mercy from God—the upward expression—and are at peace—the inward expression—then we can love others as we should—the outward expression. This *agape* love is the bond that unites believers not only to the Lord but to one another. Jesus gave us a new commandment on the evening before His crucifixion when He said, "A new command I give you: Love one another. As I have loved you, so you must also love one another. By this all men will know that you are my disciples, if you love one another" (John 13:34-35).

Apostates are void of *agape* love. As we've seen, they may be professors of Christianity, but they are not possessors of Christ. They cannot express *agape* love. The outward expression of love depends on the inward expression of peace, which depends on God's mercy—the upward expression. In order to love others, we must be at peace with ourselves, and the only way we can be at peace with ourselves is to accept mercy from the Father.

Jude began his treatise on apostasy by viewing it in a theoretical sense. Theoretically, apostates are the exact opposites of Christians. True believers are called, set aside, and kept. Apostates have not been set apart and are not being kept by Christ. Remember, apostates have received spiritual light but not spiritual life. They may have received in some way the written Word but not the living Word. They claim to be Christians, but they creep in unnoticed as impostors.

And what do apostates have? Whereas true believers have mercy from God, peace within, and love for others multiplied to them, apostates have just the opposite. That is, they have no mercy. They have not received mercy from God because they have never repented of their sins. They have no peace within because no on can have peace within when he is living a lie. They have no love for others and are self-seeking and deceitful.

Viewing apostasy theoretically reveals to us that apostates are not true believers. Never having known the mercy of God, they consequently live a lie without having real peace within. Since they do not know the Lord Jesus Christ personally, they cannot love on His level. In short, they are false prophets.

My personal prayer is that every reader who is not sure that he is kept by the Lord Jesus Christ might hear His call, know that he is loved by God, and find assurance in the fact that he can be kept by Jesus Christ through repentance of sin and faith. God offers mercy to each of us. If we accept it, we will find the peace of God that passes all understanding within our hearts and can in turn demonstrate the love of Christ to others. It is imperative that believers know who they are and what they have in Christ so they can "contend for the faith."

CHAPTER TWO
Apostasy Viewed Apologetically

Dear friends, although I was very eager to write to you about the salvation we share, I felt I had to write and urge you to contend for the faith that was once for all entrusted to the saints (Jude 3).

I. AN IRRESISTIBLE MOTIVATION
II. AN INESCAPABLE MANDATE

Having examined apostasy theoretically, Jude now deals with apostasy apologetically. *Webster's New World Dictionary* defines apologetics as "the branch of theology having to do with the defense and proofs of Christianity." Jude deals with apostasy in an apologetic sense by calling on believers to defend the faith.

Hundreds of years before Jude wrote his Epistle the psalmist asked the penetrating and probing question: "when the foundations are being destroyed, what can the righteous do?" Jude answered that question by saying that the foundations of the faith can only be kept solid when believers take seriously the admonition to "contend for the faith" entrusted to them. It is not enough to know who we are and what we have in Christ; we must know how to defend our faith. Thus, Jude 3 tells us of an irresistible motivation accompanied by an inescapable mandate.

I. AN IRRESISTIBLE MOTIVATION

Jude wrote that he fully intended the subject of his Epistle to be "the salvation we share"—that is, the redemptive work we all share as fellow believers in the Lord Jesus Christ. This would have been a fascinating and encouraging topic. We are all joint heirs with Christ. We are all of one body. We are under the same blood of Christ. We trust in the same salvation. We all have a common problem, in that we "all have sinned and fall short of the glory of God" (Romans 3:23). We all have a common provision: "For God so loved the world that he gave his one and only Son, that whoever believes in him shall not perish but have eternal life" (John 3:16). We all have a common prescription: "Everyone who calls on the name of the Lord will be saved" (Romans 10:13). These are the great truths about which Jude fully intended to write.

But Jude found it necessary to write his Epistle in another vein when the Holy Spirit changed the direction of his pen. After all, the Bible says, "men spoke from God as they were carried along by the Holy Spirit" (2 Peter 1:21). This is a good example of this truth. Jude had an irresistible motivation to write different words than he had planned to write.

Those of us who have spent a lifetime in the pulpit or with the pen know what it is like to develop a message and then have God's still, small voice direct us to another subject. Jude was attuned to the voice of God. He was overwhelmed by an urgent need to change his message. God prompted Jude to change his message, and he was sensitive and willing enough to do so. The Holy Spirit led him to leave the subject of our common salvation and to exhort us to "contend for the faith."

I can sympathize with Jude. I would much rather preach and write about the great truths of our common salvation and encourage the saints than I would to sound the alarm against apostates who eat away at the spiritual foundations of our schools, churches, and denominations. It's much more pleasant to preach, teach, or write about the book of Ephesians, for example, than that of Jude. However, we all need to be reminded that the Christian life is a battleground, not a playground.

Jude's words, "I felt I had to" suggest that he was "inwardly constrained."[1] He felt a compulsion to step to the defense of the faith. It is amazing that people today say such things as, "Let's make room in our universities and seminaries for teachers who do not believe that the first eleven chapters of Genesis are historically true and valid. Let's make room for people who discount the miracles of the Bible. Let's make room for people who do not believe that Adam and Eve were historical people." It's all too easy for us to simply ignore the problem of liberal theology, or compromise the essential tenets of our faith. Jude called on believers to defend the faith that some people are denying. He urged us to preserve the faith that some people are perverting. He exhorted us to contend for the faith that some people are corrupting.

A battle for the Bible is being fought across America today. To contend for the faith is to seriously defend our most holy faith during days when it is being subtly undermined. Many Christians are sounding the trumpet call today. Often they are accused of being intolerant and seeking to gain power, but the truth is that they are motivated by an urgency to regain the purity of their faith. When, like Jude, we become aware of apostasy, we too will have a compulsion—an irresistible motivation to "contend for the faith."

II. AN INESCAPABLE MANDATE

In an apologetic sense, we must not only develop an irresistible motivation but must take seriously the inescapable mandate, which is to "contend for the faith that was once for all entrusted to the saints." Jude reveals the content of the mandate, the completeness of the mandate, the custodians of the mandate, and the command itself.

The Content

First, Jude pointed to the content of the mandate. What is "the faith" about which Jude wrote? There is a difference between faith and "the faith". Faith is the act of believing; "the faith" is that which is believed. "The faith" is the whole body of Biblical doctrine that comprises the perfect totality of truth. "The faith" is the full and final revelation of God as we have it in the Scriptures. It is the Word of Truth that is unfolded from the book of Genesis to the book of Revelation.[2] "The faith" is the Bible—the Book of God, the Word of God! Our inescapable mandate is to contend for "the faith," and the origin of the faith is God Himself.

The Completeness

Next, Jude addressed the completeness of the mandate. He said it is "once for all" delivered to the saints. It is not merely once upon a time but once for all time![3] There can be no addition or subtraction. The Bible is a finished work. No wonder the last warning of the Bible sounds the alarm:

> I warn everyone who hears the words of the prophecy of this book: If anyone adds anything to them, God will add to him the plagues described in this book. And if anyone takes words away from this book of prophecy, God will take away from him his share in the tree of life and in the holy city, which are described in this book (Revelation 22:18-19).

It is interesting that the same phrase (once for all) used in Jude is used in Hebrews to describe our Savior's finished work on the cross.

> Then Christ would have had to suffer many times since the creation of the world. But now he has appeared once for all at the end of the ages to do away with sin by the sacrifice of himself. Just as man is destined to die once, and after that to face judgment, so Christ was sacrificed once to take away the sins of many people; and he will appear a second time, not to bare sin, but to bring salvation to those who are waiting for him (Hebrews 9:26-28).

Christ's atonement is complete. Just as the cross is a finished work, so is the Bible—the Word of God—a finished work.

One of the clearest indications of apostasy or a false cult is that people will add to or distort the teachings of the Bible. Any claim to further revelation than what is revealed in the Bible is in itself an evidence of apostasy. The faith that God entrusted once for all to the saints does not need Joseph Smith's golden tablet to be added to it eighteen hundred years later. The Bible is already complete! It is the final revelation of God. Paul wrote, "But even if we, or an angel from heaven, should preach a gospel other than the one we preached to you, let him be eternally condemned!" (Galatians 1:8)

There is not much difference between false believers adding to the Word of God and Christians adding to the Word of God. I have heard some Christians say that they have received a "word of prophecy" in some meeting that told them to do something that was diametrically opposed to the Word of God. There is no need for anyone to receive "a word of prophecy" today. There was such a need in the book of Acts because believers did not have the Bible— the final, complete, written revelation that we have today. It has been "once for all entrusted to the saints" and doesn't need additions or subtractions. It is this Word of God, "the faith . . . once for all entrusted" for which we are to contend.

"For ever, O Lord, thy word is settled in heaven" (Psalm 119:89, KJV). Someone has observed that although astronomy might discover a new star, it has never added one to the universe. Before the astronomer ever lifted his or her eye to a telescope, God had already numbered the stars and named each of them (Psalm 147:4). So it is with "the faith." It is ours to study, but it can never be added to, nor can anything be taken from it. To say that belief in the inerrancy of Scripture was acceptable for the founders of many of our denominational universities and seminaries but is not necessary for their current leaders is absurd. We are called to "contend for the faith that was once for all entrusted to the saints." We live in an age when people add to the Bible and take away from it. Both practices are wrong. The Bible says that such actions are clear indications of the last days. The Book of God is the truth, and if we love God we must contend for the faith as long as we have our breath.

The Custodians

Jude goes on to refer to the custodians of the mandate. "The faith" has been entrusted to "the saints"—to you and me! The faith has not been invested in human institutions, organizations, or even churches. We have in our care, in our custody, the Word of the living God. That is why we cannot stand idly by and watch the Bible being ridiculed and torn apart by liberal theologians. God has called us to be guardians of His Word. We are to "contend for the faith that was once for all entrusted to the saints."

Paul exhorted young Timothy, saying, "And the things you have heard me say in the presence of many witnesses, entrust to reliable men who will also be qualified to teach others" (2 Timothy 2:2). You and I would not have the Word of God today if it were not for the faithful believers down through the centuries who guarded and passed on this precious treasure. When we think of our spiritual forefathers through the centuries who gave their lives to contend for God's Word, we recognize our responsibility to contend earnestly for it today. Perhaps Isaac Watts said it best when he penned these words:

> Am I a soldier of the cross?
> A foll'wer of the lamb?
> And shall I fear to own His cause
> Or blush to speak His name?
>
> Must I be carried to the skies
> On flow'ry beds of ease,
> While others fought to win the prize
> And sailed thru bloody seas?

We are custodians of this treasure, the faith we call the Bible. That is why we must take seriously our call to stand for the Word of God. Each of us should ask ourselves, *How will this faith be passed on to the next generation if it were up to me?*

I trust we all see the importance of this point. Every generation is important, and the baton has been passed to us. We must hand down this faith to the next generation—uncorrupted, unperverted, and still possessing its original truth. That is why we must stand firm in the battle for the Bible today. It is "the faith"—"once for all entrusted"—"to the saints." It was delivered to the saints by God, not discovered by the saints! It comes from God and not from man, and our responsibility is to contend for it.

The Command

Dealing with apostasy in an apologetic sense also includes the command regarding "the faith." The Bible commands us to "contend for the faith." How can we earnestly contend for this sacred trust that is once for all entrusted to us? Let me suggest four ways: love the faith, learn the faith, live the faith, and finally loose the faith.

First, we should love the faith. This is where our defense begins. Men and women give their lives for that which they love. Hundreds of thousands of Americans have fought in wars and other conflicts because of their love for liberty. Likewise, we cannot contend for something or someone we do not love. Thus the first step in learning to contend for the faith is to love the faith, the Word of God.

We cannot contend for the faith if we do not have a respect and love for the Word of God. The way to start loving God's written Word is to grow to love Christ, the living Word. The only way we can do this is by being born again. We who are custodians of the faith must first of all love the faith by submitting ourselves to the Lord Jesus Christ. Apostates deny Him, but Christians receive Him.

Once we love the faith, then we should learn the faith. It is very difficult to defend something about which we know nothing. For example, I spent four undergraduate years at Texas Christian University as a pre-law student. My life's dream (before the Lord called me during my senior year to the high calling of the ministry) was to be a trial lawyer. So I know enough about law to know that a lawyer in a courtroom would not do a good job defending a case that he had never studied. Yet many believers who say that they love the faith have never learned the faith. They never study the Bible—the Book of God.

What do you suppose would happen this coming Sunday morning if the typical preacher in the typical church asked his parishioners to turn to the book of Hezekiah? Sadly, I fear the majority would start looking for it even though there is no such book in the Bible! Biblical illiteracy in the pulpit and in the pew is one of the tragedies of our day. There is no excuse for Christians not to know the Word of God. God admonishes us to "do your best to present yourself to God as one approved, a workman who does not need to be ashamed and who correctly handles the word of truth" (2 Timothy 2:15). "All scripture is useful for teaching, rebuking, correcting, and training in righteousness, so that the man of God may be thoroughly equipped for every good work" (2 Timothy 3:16-17).

As believers, we should make certain we can defend our faith in three vital areas: the inerrancy of Scripture, the deity of Christ, and salvation by grace through faith. We can never contend for the faith until we learn the faith.

How do we take seriously this inescapable mandate to contend for the faith? We begin when we love the faith. We continue when we learn the faith. Third, we should live the faith. The final argument for the validity of our faith is not the argument of our lips but the argument of our lives. The greatest argument for Christianity is the life of the believer. Living the faith involves standing unashamedly in support of the Bible. Not everyone will like us when we take this stand for Christ. People will accuse us of being narrow-minded and mean. They will accuse us of trying to break fellowship. When we really live the faith, we should not expect this world, which so viciously crucified our Lord Jesus Christ, to accept us with open arms.

One way people can live the faith today is by supporting Bible-believing, soul-saving churches. We should all be involved in churches that stand for the faith. During my early years of ministry I used to tell new Christians to attend the church of their choice—but no more! Now I tell people to bury their lives in a Bible-believing, Bible-teaching, disciple-making church.

Part of our problem today is that many good people attend many bad churches. How many times have I heard them say, "I just hate to leave my church because our family has been here for so many years. Our children were baptized here thirty years ago. We were married here in this church. Mother's funeral was in this church." Friend, as true believers we cannot contend for the faith in an apostate church. Yes, some people stay in a church because their grandmother is buried in the church cemetery out back. But the church of grandmother's day may have been quite different from the church of today. If the truth were known, if grandmother could, she would probably get up and get out of there...and so should many people today who are true believers.

Those who support the work of apostate churches will one day answer to God for their actions. These are the only people from whom the Bible says we should "turn away." Apostate churches are going to produce a whole group of young adults who know nothing about Scripture. We can contend for the faith only when we live the faith.

It is important at this point for us to realize that in contending for the faith we must guard against being contentious.[4] Paul admonished us in the Epistle of Ephesians to "speak the truth in love" (Ephesians 4:15). As believers, we are to contend for the faith without being contentious. The Bible says we are to do it with a loving spirit, not with a bitter, hateful, arrogant, or haughty spirit. We live the faith by being Christlike. Unfortunately many people speak the truth but do not do it in love.

We are to speak the truth not just to prove that others are wrong and to expose them, but to win them to Christ. The best way I know to win people to Christ is to speak the truth in love. If I know someone whose view is contrary to Scripture, should I rush out and verbally attack him? Some Christians obviously think I should. Perhaps the person is a babe in Christ and holds a wrong view simply because he or she has never been taught. Maybe he or she has just been fooled by false teaching. Thus I should have a sense of compassion for this person and should speak the truth in love. Real truth produces passion and love. The Bible says that when Jesus saw the crowds "he had compassion on them, because they were harassed and helpless, like sheep without a shepherd" (Matthew 9:36).

Many of God's solid soldiers are paying a great price in defending the faith today. In many denominations those who seek to keep their thumbs in the spiritual dike in order to hold back the floodwaters of apostasy are branded as mean fundamentalists because they will not compromise the Word of God. In my own denomination (Southern Baptist Convention), the Peace Committee that was appointed to seek solutions to the current controversy concerning the Bible has revealed that some seminary professors do not believe in the historicity of the first eleven chapters of Genesis. Other professors discount many of the Bible's miracles. One of the ways we live the faith is by standing up for the Bible, and that means we cannot sit idly by and watch churches and denominations follow a spirit of apostasy.

Finally, we contend for the faith by loosing the faith. By this I mean we must be about the business of sharing the faith. Often people say, "Keep the faith, baby." No! We are to give it away! The late Paul Little stated this truth best in his classic volume, *How to Give Away Your Faith*. If we are not giving away our faith, maybe we should give it up.

The truth is, we cannot loose the faith if we do not live the faith. We cannot live the faith if we do not learn the faith. And we cannot learn the faith if we do not love the faith. That is why the Lord Jesus said that the greatest commandment of all was to "love the Lord your God with all your heart" (Matthew 22:37a). We need to love the faith, learn the faith, live the faith, and loose the faith, and in so doing join together in this swelling chorus:

> I love to tell the story!
> 'Twill be my theme in glory—
> To tell the old, old story
> Of Jesus and his love.
> (A. Catherine Hankey)

In viewing apostasy apologetically, we recognize our responsibility as true believers in contending for the faith. Like Jude, we should have the Holy Spirit's irresistible motivation welling up within us, and we should also take seriously our inescapable mandate. We are to contend for the faith, the Word of God that God delivered once for all to us, the saints.

How can we contend for this faith? By loving the faith, learning the faith, living the faith, and loosing the faith. Unless we take this mandate seriously, we will have no one else to blame but ourselves if the foundations are destroyed.

CHAPTER THREE
Apostasy Viewed Synthetically

For certain men whose condemnation was written about long ago have secretly slipped in among you. They are godless men, who change the grace of our God into a license for immorality and deny Jesus Christ our only Sovereign and Lord (Jude 4).

I. THE APOSTATE'S DECEITFULNESS
II. THE APOSTATE'S DEVOTION
III. THE APOSTATE'S DEMEANOR
IV. THE APOSTATE'S DOCTRINE

T he city of Fort Lauderdale is primarily known for its beautiful beaches and miles of waterways within the city limits. It is billed as the "Venice of America." Many people do not know however that Fort Lauderdale is the home of one of the world's largest swap shops! Having passed this swap shop a thousand times, one day I decided to stop in and browse. I walked by one booth and could not believe my eyes. Beautiful watches were being sold for a fraction of their retail cost. Remembering my wife's birthday, I purchased a watch, which normally would have cost several hundred dollars, for only fifteen dollars. I rushed home and proudly presented it to her as a birthday gift.

An interesting thing happened later that evening during dinner. When she looked down at her watch, to her surprise the second hand was going "berserk." And then it happened...the beautiful watch stopped dead in its tracks. To my chagrin, even though the watch looked like the real thing, it was synthetic. It did not stand up under pressure. No matter how real its outward appearance looked, it was a fake.

This illustration applies to the apostate. In verse 4, Jude revealed him for who he is—a phony, a synthetic saint. He may look like the real thing, but he is not. *Webster's New World Dictionary* defines *synthetic* as, "not real or genuine; artificial."

Jesus emphasized this point when He told the parable of the sower in Luke 8.[1] He revealed that the apostate is like the seed sown on rocky ground. This man, when he hears the Word, receives it with joy but develops no roots. For a while he believes, but during the time of temptation he "falls away" (Luke 8:13). The verb form used in "fall away" is the verb form of "apostasy."[2] An apostate receives the Word, believes it for a while, and then falls away.

The secret of this passage lies in the careful choice of words used in the original Greek. Referring to the stony ground—the hearers who "receive the word" in Luke 8:13—the Holy Spirit used the word *dekomai*. A different word, for "receive," *paradekoamai*, is used to describe the good ground—hearers who also "receive the word" (Mark 4:20). This is a much stronger word that indicates they welcome the Word into their hearts. The stony-ground hearers, on the other hand, only do so superficially.

Those who fall away from the truth of God have no spiritual roots. Consequently they have no fruit, no life in Christ. An absence of spiritual fruit reflects an absence of genuine evidence of the Christian life. An apostate may have received light but not life. Jude expressed this truth later in his Epistle: "These men are blemishes at your love feasts, eating with you without the slightest qualm— shepherds who feed only themselves. They are clouds without rain, blown along by the wind; autumn trees, without fruit and uprooted—twice dead" (Jude 12).

The apostate knows the truth but does not apply it. He "accepts" God's revelation as true but does not make a sincere commitment to it. He is a synthetic saint, not a sincere saint. A truly born-again person cannot become an apostate. Though he or she may fall into error or into indifference, he cannot fall away from the faith. In the beginning and the conclusion of his Epistle, Jude explicitly re- minded us that Jesus is able to "keep" true believers forever.

Jude wasted no time in identifying apostates in a synthetic sense. He described them in regard to their deceitfulness, their devotion, their demeanor, and their doctrine.

I. THE APOSTATE'S DECEITFULNESS

The Greek word rendered "secretly slipped in" (4) carries with it the idea of slipping in through the backdoor. The word means "to steal in under cover."[3] It is also used to describe someone who slips secretly into a country from which he has been expelled. It is also the word picture of an alligator lying on the bank of a river, then slithering into the river so subtly, secretly, and silently, that it doesn't even make a ripple in the water. Jude said that these deceitful, synthetic saints creep into denominations, churches, and schools in a similar manner. They worm their way into Sunday school classes, into choirs, into pews, into classrooms, and into pulpits. Jesus warned about apostates and their deceitfulness when He said, "Watch out for false prophets. They come to you in sheep's clothing, but inwardly they are ferocious wolves" (Matthew 7:15). Apostates are destructive. They destroy schools, churches, and denominations.

Of the first one hundred colleges founded in America, eighty-eight of them, including Harvard, were founded in order to propagate the gospel of the Lord Jesus Christ. I recently heard some interesting facts regarding the founding of Harvard in 1636. During the early days Harvard students were to follow three basic rules. First, all students were to consider it the main end of their studies to know God and eternal life through the Lord Jesus Christ. Second, recognizing that the Lord gave wisdom, every student was by prayer to seek wisdom of God. Third, everyone was to exercise himself in the reading of the Scriptures twice a day, so that he could give an account of his profession.

Clearly, every student at Harvard was to be a student of the Word of God. Every student was to pray for wisdom. Every student was to trust Christ as Lord and Savior. This was the aim of the school in its early days. Other great universities of the time had similar aims. The first president of Princeton said, "Cursed be all learning that is contrary to the cross of Christ." I wonder if the presidents of these major universities would say the same thing today?

What happened to many American schools that were founded on the fundamentals of our faith? Jude reveals the answer in Jude 4: apostates "secretly slipped in" to these Christian schools. That is why we must contend for the faith in our denominations today.

We have watched other denominations become apostate. Once they were great and strong, and produced missionaries who went around the world. But now many denominations are dead or dying. That is why a battle for the Bible is going on in the church today.

Who would have ever dreamed that a few years ago a Baptist professor would call Charles Darwin "one of my scientific heroes"? Who would have ever dreamed that a Baptist university professor would claim that creation theory, if given equal time in the classroom, would "destroy all of science"? Who would have ever imagined that some Baptist theologians would deny many of the miracles of the Old Testament? When we begin to deny the miracles of the Old Testament, it is not long before we deny the miracles of the New Testament, which eventually leads us to deny the resurrection of our Lord Jesus Christ.

We have come a long way during the last several generations. Dr. L. R. Scarborough, who was the second president of what is now the largest theological seminary in the world—Southwestern Baptist Theological Seminary in Fort Worth—related an incredible conversation he had with the founding president, his predecessor, Dr. B. H. Carroll. In his book, *Gospel Messages,* which was published in 1922, Dr. Scarborough told of going to Dr. Carroll's room a few days before he died. He wrote that Carroll looked forty feet high as he pulled himself up from the pillow, looked into Scarborough's face, and said:

> My boy, on this seminary hill, orthodoxy, the old truth, is making one of its last stands. I want to deliver to you a charge and I do it in the blood of Jesus Christ. You will be elected the president of this seminary. I want you, if there ever comes heresy in your faculty, to take it to your faculty. If they don't hear you take it to the trustees. If they don't hear you, take it to the conventions that appointed them. If they won't hear you, take it to the common Baptists. They will hear you.

He then concluded, "I charge you in the name of the Lord Jesus Christ to keep it lashed to the old Gospel of Jesus Christ."

Scarborough then replied, "As long as I have influence in that institution, by the grace of God, I will stand by the old book."[4]

Men and women such as these have played an important role in

forming America's spiritual roots. They "contend for the faith that
was once for all entrusted to the saints."

II. The Apostate's Devotion

Jude then moves from the apostate's deceitfulness to reveal to
us their devotion. In verse 4, he used the phrase "godless men,"
which means men who lack reverential awe toward God. It is a lack
of what we call "the fear of God." These ungodly men have a form
of godliness but deny its power (2 Timothy 3:5). They stand in
contrast to godly men who walk with God and know God.

Jude did not write about outward appearances here. He did not
describe people who are openly and outwardly ungodly, nor
people who are blatantly ungodly. Jude was writing about men's
hearts. Remember, apostates look and act like Christians. They
may appear to be good in the eyes of other people. All apostates
talk about God and use the right terminology, but their hearts are
far from Him. The ungodly men Jude described may be gifted,
courteous, gentle, good, and even generous in the eyes of others.
But in the eyes of God, they are "godless."

Paul warned his young son in the ministry about these individuals when he told Timothy to "turn away" from those who had a
form of godliness but denied its power. These are the only people
in the Bible from whom Jesus says we should withdraw fellowship.
Paul warned about these synthetic saints when he wrote, "For the
time will come when men will not put up with sound doctrine.
Instead, to suit their own desires, they will gather around them a
great number of teachers to say what their itching ears want to
hear. They will turn their ears away from the truth and turn aside
to myths" (2 Timothy 4:3-4).

Apostasy began in the Garden of Eden when Satan questioned
the Word of God. Eve knew the Word to be true, but Satan planted
the seed of doubt by saying, "Did God really say." (Genesis 3:1). And
Eve, knowing the truth, moved away from it. This is the spirit of
apostasy, which continues today through the mouths of liberal
professors and preachers who question the Word of God using the
same words, "Did God really say?"

Although apostates may claim to love the Lord Jesus, they do not obey Him. They claim to serve Him, but they are really serving their own selfish interests. They are in many churches. They are leaders in many schools. The devotion of apostates is summed up in the words of Titus 1:16: "They claim to know God, but by their actions they deny him. They are detestable, disobedient, and unfit for doing anything good."

III. THE APOSTATE'S DEMEANOR

When we view apostasy in a synthetic sense, we see the apostates' deceitfulness, devotion, and also their demeanor. They "change the grace of our God into a license for immorality" (Jude 4). The men Jude described do not arrogantly flaunt their sins, although they do evil deeds without any shame or sense of decency. These men say that they can sin all they like and God will forgive them. They think that the more they sin, the greater God's grace toward them will be. They pervert the doctrine of grace, using it to justify sin. In effect, they change the grace of God into lewdness. They take our liberty in Christ and turn it into a license to sin! Remember, grace is God's "unmerited favor." When this precious Biblical truth is perverted into a license to sin, apostasy has set in. This is one of the most distinguishing characteristics of apostasy. No person can believe God gives license to sin without denying the Lord Jesus Christ.

Let's say that a professing Christian begins to think, *I can do what I please, go where I want, and indulge in my fleshly desires because I am under the grace of God.* Perhaps he or she then says something like this: "I am just a human being; I am vulnerable. God's grace is big enough to cover my sin; He'll forgive me. He is the God of great grace." I am afraid for anyone who says something like that, because such a person knows nothing of the grace of God.

Jude wrote that apostates turn the grace of God into "lewdness"(NKJV). This word means "an absence of moral restraint." The Greek word, *aselgeia,* describes a person who is so lost to decency, honor, and shame that he or she doesn't care who knows about his sin. He has no feelings of guilt. Apostates assume that their privileges in the faith somehow put them above the moral responsibility of the Word that binds true believers to lifestyles of godliness and purity. This is apostasy in its worst form.

The grace of God however does not lead us to sin. Interestingly, the Bible teaches that a person who truly knows the grace of God will act quite contrary to this. The apostle Paul wrote:

> For the grace of God that brings salvation has appeared to all men. It teaches us to say "No" to ungodliness and worldly passions, and to live self-controlled, upright and godly lives in this present age, while we wait for the blessed hope—the glorious appearing of our great God and Savior, Jesus Christ (Titus 2:11-13).

The grace of God will lead us to deny ungodliness and worldly lusts. It will lead us to live righteously and godly.

The writer of Hebrews solemnly warns those who turn the grace of God into a license for immorality. "How much more severely do you think a man deserves to be punished who has trampled the Son of God under foot, who has treated as an unholy thing the blood of the covenant that sanctified him, and who has insulted the Spirit of grace?" (Hebrews 10:29) It is dangerous to insult the Spirit of grace by using our liberty in Christ as a license to sin.

In a synthetic sense, apostates are deceitful. Their devotion is ungodly, and their demeanor attempts to turn the grace of God into licentiousness. Jude wasted no time nor minced any words in identifying these synthetic saints. Next he went on to reveal their doctrine.

IV. THE APOSTATE'S DOCTRINE

Continuing his description, Jude wrote that apostates "deny Jesus Christ our only sovereign and Lord." Now do not misunderstand a key point. They do not deny Jesus with their lips. Remember, they have "secretly slipped in." They profess to be Christians. Rather, they deny Him with their lives.[5] Here is the root of the problem. Their demeanor results from their doctrine. They deny the *only* Lord God and our Lord Jesus Christ. There are not several lords, any more than there are several ways to Heaven. There is only one Lord, whom they deny.

Why were Christians thrown to the lions when many other religious people whom the Romans conquered did not meet a similar fate? The Christians insisted that there was only one Lord. They would not bow down to the image of Caesar and say, "Caesar is Lord."

In Rome there is a building called the Pantheon. One of the best-preserved Roman ruins, it was built in 27 B.C. to serve as the temple to all the gods. In this building there were niches around the walls for all the gods and goddesses of people conquered by the Romans. In this way the Romans appeased their captives. There was, for example, a niche for the god Jupiter. His followers could come into the Pantheon and worship him. Next to Jupiter was a niche for Juno. In niche after niche after niche gods were placed around the walls.

When the Romans conquered the Christians, they said, "We are going to give you a niche for Jesus." But the Christians said, "No! There is only one Lord. There will be no niche for Jesus." And they gave their lives for that truth. They were ripped apart by lions and burned at the stake because they insisted that Jesus Christ was the "only sovereign and Lord."

That is why it is so nauseating today to hear professors in our schools deny our Lord Jesus Christ. Some time ago, a Baptist professor featured on a national television talk show affirmed the fact that some of his friends who had rejected Jesus Christ would be in Heaven and that he would see them there. However, the Bible says, "there is no other name under heaven...by which we must be saved" (Acts 4:12). Of course that name is the name of Jesus!

That is why it is so heartbreaking to hear professors espousing universalist philosophies and doctrines, many of which discount a belief in Hell. In the past, most people who had a spirit of apostasy simply denied our only Lord with their lives and not their lips. Today people are becoming far more blatant in denying Him with their lips. We should all remember that Jesus himself warned, "Whoever disowns me before men, I will disown him before my Father in heaven" (Matthew 10:33).

God hates apostasy! One mark of apostates is that they commit the greatest sin of all: they deny our only Lord Jesus Christ. They deny Him as Master (Lord). They deny Him as Mediator even though He is the only one who can bring sinners into a right relationship with God. They also deny Him as Messiah (Christ).

Note the definite downward progression here. First, apostates become ungodly in the sense that they have no fear of God, no reverential awe. Therefore they pervert the precious doctrine of grace and use it as an excuse to sin. Lacking any fear of God, it is then easy for them to turn the grace of God into a license for immorality, which leads to their outright denial of the only Lord and sovereign, Jesus Christ.

What the devil could not do from without, he is seeking to do from within through deceitful, synthetic saints who creep in unnoticed. Their devotion is ungodly. Their demeanor gives them away. Their doctrine denies Jesus Christ, our only Lord. The root of the problem in many churches today is that we have ceased to recognize the wolves in sheep's clothing that have crept in unnoticed.

CHAPTER FOUR
Apostasy Viewed Apathetically

Though you already know all this, I want to remind you that the Lord delivered his people out of Egypt, but later destroyed those who did not believe. And the angels who did not keep their positions of authority but abandoned their own home—these he has kept in darkness, bound with everlasting chains for judgment on the great Day. In a similar way, Sodom and Gomorrah and the surrounding towns gave themselves up to sexual immorality and perversion. They serve as an example of those who suffer the punishment of eternal fire (Jude 5-7).

I. The Danger of Losing Our Victory
II. The Danger of Losing Our Vocation
III. The Danger of Losing Our Virtue

When the foundations are being destroyed, what can the righteous do?" (Psalm 11:3) The real problem in dealing with apostasy today is the problem of apathy, which *Webster's New World Dictionary* defines as "lack of interest; indifference." Denominations are dying, not simply because apostates have crept in but because godly men and women have been apathetic and have done nothing to stop them.

Jude reminds us, in verse 5, of what we already know. "Though you already know all this," he wrote, "I want to remind you." He called us to remember. Why? Because we have forgotten! Many of us are prone to be apathetic and say, "So what?" Thus the problem is not only apostasy in the pulpit but apathy in the pew.

The book of Jude calls us to look at and learn from the past so that we might become overcomers in the future. In order to awaken us out of our apathy, the writer used three illustrations to warn us. He illustrated the truth of apathy in the pew by relating the experiences of the Israelites, the angels, and Sodom. They all have one thing in common. They fell! Israel lost its victory, the angels lost their vocation, and Sodom lost its virtue. Likewise, we also are in danger of losing our victory, our vocation, and our virtue.

I. THE DANGER OF LOSING OUR VICTORY

In considering the first lesson from the past, Jude called out, as it were, "Remember the Israelites!" Because of unbelief, they lost their victory and were not able to enter the promised land. The Epistle of Jude seeks to arouse the church from its apathetic slumber and to warn us of the danger of losing our victory. The author called us to remember because we so quickly forget and grow apathetic. He reminded us that we "already know all this." What Jude told us is based on what we already know. We should never assume that because people hear something, they will act on it. We all need to be reminded of what we know.

The Israelites' experience about which Jude wrote took place at Kadesh-Barnea. Shortly after leaving Egyptian bondage, they passed through the Red Sea and watched the pursuing Egyptian army drown. Moses led them to the very portals of the promised land at Kadesh-Barnea, where they sent twelve spies to spy out the land. Ten spies came back with a majority report saying that because of the giants in the land and the walled cities there was no possibility of conquest. The other two spies, Joshua and Caleb, came back with a minority report saying that even though what the others had said was true, they could conquer the land because God had promised it to them and would fight for them. The Israelites voted to accept the majority report and consequently spent the next forty years wandering aimlessly in the wilderness.

Amazingly, the Israelites did not believe that the same God who had parted the Red Sea, destroyed Pharaoh's army before their eyes, provided manna from heaven every morning, led them with a cloud by day and a pillar of fire by night, and provided water from the rock could also enable them to overcome the land of Canaan after He had promised to do so all along. How tragic was their unbelief! They forgot what God had done for them. Some of us are no different. We cannot believe God's plans for our future even though we have seen Him do so much in the past.

Paul did his part to awaken us from our apathy when he wrote:

> For I do not want you to be ignorant of the fact, brothers, that our forefathers were all under the cloud and they all passed through the sea. They were all baptized into Moses in the cloud and in the sea. They all ate the same spiritual food and drank the same spiritual drink; for they drank from the spiritual rock that accompanied them, and that rock was Christ (1 Corinthians 10:1-4).

The Israelites perished because of their unbelief. The account is detailed in the Book of Numbers:

> That night all the people of the community raised their voices and wept aloud. All the Israelites grumbled against Moses and Aaron, and the whole assembly said to them, "If only we had died in Egypt! Or in this desert!" (Numbers 14:1-2)

God then answered their prayer:

> So tell them, 'As surely as I live, declares the Lord, I will do to you the very things I heard you say: In this desert your bodies will fall—every one of you twenty years old or more who was counted in the census and who has grumbled against me. Your children will be shepherds here for forty years, suffering for your unfaithfulness, until the last of your bodies lies in the desert' (Numbers 14:28-29,33).

Jude said that we had best remember this experience, or we too might lose our spiritual victory. The Israelites wandered for forty years until that generation—all those who were more than twenty years of age at Kadesh-Barnea—died. Only "Caleb son of Jephunneh the Kenizzite and Joshua son of Nun" could enter the promised land, "for they followed the Lord wholeheartedly" (Numbers 32:12).

The writer of Hebrews pointedly told us that this punishment happened because of the Israelites' unbelief:

Who were they who heard and rebelled? Were they not all those Moses led out of Egypt? And with whom was he angry for forty years? Was it not with those who sinned, whose bodies fell in the desert? And to whom did God swear that they would never enter his rest if not to those who disobeyed? So we see that they were not able to enter, because of their unbelief (Hebrews 3:16-19).[1]

Jude urged us to "remember the Israelites!" They lost their victory. They were not permitted to live in the promised land. They missed the blessing of God. Do we Christians see the warning here? There is a possibility of losing our victory, of becoming what Paul called a "castaway." That is, we could receive no crown, and only be saved though as by fire (see 1 Corinthians 3:14-15).

Jude does not stand alone in Scripture with his warning to believers who fall into unbelief. John also tells us that believers can commit a sin unto death. "If anyone sees his brother commit a sin that does not lead to death, he should pray, and God will give him life. I refer to those whose sin does not lead to death. There is a sin that leads to death. I am not saying that he should pray about that" (1 John 5:16). Ananias and Sapphira are perfect examples of the sin unto death (Acts 5:1-11).

We have so many privileges and victories as born-again believers. What a tragedy to lose a life of blessing. Jude warned us that God deals sternly with those who turn their back on Him in unbelief after having seen Him use such wonderful power. There is a word of warning here for anyone or any church that has received the blessing of God and comes to a Kadesh-Barnea. The same God who got the Israelites through the Red Sea can get us through our struggles and into the "promised land."

The whole experience of the Israelites was recorded for our benefit. Paul wrote, "Now these things occurred as examples to keep us from setting our hearts on evil things as they did" (1 Corinthians 10:6). The events that happened to them are examples to us. He then added, "These things happened to them as examples and were written down as warnings for us, on whom the fulfillment of the ages has come" (1 Corinthians 10:11). The great lesson here is that even though God has saved us, He reserves the right to discipline us if we become guilty of unbelief and the sin to which it leads.[2] God takes away the victory of those who think they can continue in sin and get away with it, just as He took away the Israelites' victory.

II. THE DANGER OF LOSING OUR VOCATION

In considering the second lesson from the past, Jude referred to angels who lost their position—their vocation. The nature of their sin is revealed throughout Scripture. Note carefully that verse 7 says that the sin of the angels was similar to the sin of Sodom. What was the sin of Sodom? It was "sexual immorality and perversion." If the sin of these angels was like the sin of Sodom and Gomorrah some contend that Jude was referring to an experience that happened in the days before the flood.[3]

> When men began to increase in number on the earth and daughters were born to them, the sons of God saw that the daughters of men were beautiful and they married any of them they chose. Then the Lord said, "My Spirit will not contend with man forever, for he is mortal; his days will be a hundred and twenty years." The Nephilim were on the earth in those days—and also afterward—when the sons of God went to the daughters of men and had children by them. They were the heroes of old, men of renown (Genesis 6:1-4).

The term "sons of God" is translated "angels" in the Septuagint (the Greek translation of the original Hebrew text). Also, the Hebrew rendering of "sons of God" is used exclusively in the Old Testament to describe angels. What some understand from these verses is that fallen angels came to earth during the days of Noah and had sexual relations with women, thus producing a race of giants that the Bible refers to as *Nephilim*. This was one reason God destroyed the world using the flood during Noah's day.

By their volition, these angelic creatures left their lofty positions in the realm of the heavenlies, and in leaving they lost their vocation. They left their high calling when they rebelled against God. The angels to which Jude alluded in verse 6 were not just ordinary fallen angels or demons. Ordinary demons are not in chains at the present time. The once bright and shining angels about whom Jude wrote are "kept in darkness, bound with everlasting chains."

There are two categories of fallen angels that are referred to as demons in Scripture. Some of them are unchained and have access to the high places and bodies of unsaved people. We know this from Ephesians 6:12, which tells us that we struggle against "rulers, against the authorities, against the powers of this dark world and against the spiritual forces of evil in the heavenly realms." There are many occasions in the New Testament when these demons inhabited the bodies of unsaved people. Yet another group of demons is presently in chains. Not only does Jude speak of them, but Peter does as well: "God did not spare angels when they sinned, but sent them to hell, putting them into gloomy dungeons to be held for judgment" (2 Peter 2:4).

Two things brought about the downfall of these angels and the loss of their vocation. First, their pride caused them to fall. They wanted to be "like the Most High" (Isaiah 14:14). Also, their lust played a key role. The doom of these fallen angels is sealed. They lost their vocation and cut themselves off from everything that might have been theirs. They lost it all through unbelief and pride.[4]

The point is, apostasy is serious. Once we let pride and lust rule our lives, we lose our high calling. Jude warned against this in these verses, lest we all meet a fate similar to that of the fallen angels and lose our vocation, our high calling. Once angels of light, the fallen angels are today in chains of darkness. What a tragedy when sin is allowed to defeat us.

How many men and women today have lost their privileges as believers, and their positions of service, because of their sin? What is the church doing today to maintain its high position? By and large, it sits by apathetically while Jude warns us of the danger of not only losing our victory but our vocation. His words shout loudly, "Remember the angels!" They were created for a high position and lost it because of pride and lust.

We can no longer sit by in apathy. The Bible says, "If one of you should wander from the truth...someone should bring him back" (James 5:19). Jude addressed apostasy caused by apathy by calling us to wake up and remember! There is a danger of losing our victory and our vocation. Judgment is coming.

III. THE DANGER OF LOSING OUR VIRTUE

Next, Jude pointed out another lesson from the past. According to Jude, the church needs to wake up and remember Sodom. There is a danger that we might lose our virtue. We can lose a lot, but if we still have our virtue we can hold our heads high. We must guard against losing our virtue.

Christ prophesied that the last days would be similar to the days of Lot when He said:

> It was the same in the days of Lot. People were eating and drinking, buying and selling, planting and building. But the day Lot left Sodom, fire and sulfur rained down from heaven and destroyed them all. It will be just like this on the day the Son of Man is revealed (Luke 17:28-30).

The account about which Jude wrote is recorded in Genesis 19. Two angelic visitors, evidently in human form, came to visit Lot. Lot invited them into his home for the night, and a crowd soon gathered outside his house. The men of Sodom wanted the two visitors to be brought outside so that they might engage in homosexual acts with them. One can hardly believe it, but in a vain attempt to defuse the situation, Lot offered his two virgin daughters to the crowd! (Genesis 19:8) However the crowd did not want female companionship. All they could think about was having sex with the two men. As the story unfolds, God struck the crowd with blindness but not even that stopped them. They continued to grope in the dark for the door handle in order to find the celestial visitors.

No wonder Jude warned us to remember Sodom! When people go too far in sin, God gives them over to their sin. Paul alluded to this in Romans 1 when he wrote:

> Although they claimed to be wise, they became fools and exchanged the glory of the immortal God for images made to look like mortal man and birds and animals and reptiles. Therefore God gave them over in the sinful desires of their hearts to sexual impurity for the degrading of their bodies with one another. They exchanged the truth of God for a lie,

and worshiped and served created things rather than the Creator—who is forever praised. Amen. Because of this, God gave them over to shameful lusts. Even their women exchanged natural relations for unnatural ones. In the same way the men also abandoned natural relations with women and were inflamed with lust for one another. Men committed indecent acts with other men, and received in themselves the due penalty for their perversion. Furthermore, since they did not think it worthwhile to retain the knowledge of God, he gave them over to a depraved mind, to do what ought not to be done (Romans 1:22-28).

This was the sin of Sodom. The Sodomites lost their virtue. God does not sit idly by, smiling at people's sin. He "rained down burning sulfur on Sodom and Gomorrah" and "overthrew those cities" (Genesis 19:24-25).

Nearly two thousand years have passed since Jude warned us to remember Sodom! Today unbelievers go right on indulging in sin. However, we need to remember that Jude's words were not written to unbelievers but to believers, those who have been "called" by God, who are "loved" by the Father and "kept" by the Lord Jesus Christ. These words were written so that we might not lose our virtue, but unless we remember them, we have no hope.

This warning should make every Christian an earnest soul winner and defender of the faith. The God who did what the Bible says He did to the Israelites, the angels, and the Sodomites can and possibly will do it again! Why should we think that we can sin and get away with it? Dr. Billy Graham has said, "If God doesn't punish America, he will have to apologize to Sodom and Gomorrah."[5]

The fabric of our society is unraveling before our eyes. We had better sound the cry with Jude, loudly and clearly: "Remember Sodom!" In the fall of 1986, the Attorney General's Commission on Pornography in America published its report. Anyone who has read that report should heed the warnings found in the book of Jude. Under the protection of so-called first amendment rights, sexual materials are being published in our nation today that would make even the inhabitants of Sodom blush. Dr. James Dobson, a member of the Commission, reported, "The mainstream of explicit material sold in sex shops today, focuses on rape, incest, defecation, urination, mutilation, bestiality, vomiting, enemas, homosexuality, and sadomasochistic activity." We may point an accusing finger at Sodom, but this is America about which Dobson is speaking! And by and large, the church sits by and watches in total apathy. This is a tragedy!

Is it not time for men today to stand in the pulpit and preach the Word fearlessly and faithfully as Jude exhorts us to do? Is it not time for us to awaken from our apathy and exhort one another to remember the Israelites, lest we lose our victory? Is it not time for us to remember the angels, lest we lose our vocation? Is it not time for us to remember Sodom, lest we lose our virtue?

So many of us today are apathetic because we have been infiltrated by apostates who have "secretly slipped in" to the classroom and pulpit. Under the guise of being true believers, these synthetic saints have turned the grace of God into a license for immorality and have rocked the church to sleep in apathy. But God has His ways of moving them off the scene. They begin by losing their victory. Then they lose their vocation and finally they lose their virtue.

Israel's sin was unbelief. The angels' sin was rebellion. Sodom's sin was sensual indulgence. These three sins characterize apostates. Apostates do not live by faith, they reject authority, and they cannot control their sensual passions. Consequently, what do they do? They creep into churches and schools and try to make others believe that they are true believers.

Apostasy in the pulpit is not the only problem we face today. It is coupled with apathy in the pew. May we never forget our high calling and the Christ of Calvary. It's no wonder the songwriter, Jennie Evelyn Hussey, wrote:

> King of my life, I crown Thee now,
> Thine shall the glory be;
> Lest I forget Thy thorn crowned brow,
> Lead me to Calvary.

> Lest I forget Gethsemane;
> Lest I forget Thine agony;
> Lest I forget Thy love for me
> Lead me to Calvary.

One wonderful attribute of God is that He never forgets us, although we may forget Him. He is never apathetic toward us! We know this because He said, "Can a mother forget the baby at her breast and have no compassion on the child she has borne? Though she may forget, I will not forget you. See, I have engraved you on the palms of my hands; your walls are ever before me" (Isaiah 49:15-16).

Jude called us to remember because we so easily forget and sink into apathy. Down through the corridors of the centuries, his words echo into our hearts today. Hear him as he shouts, "Don't lose your victory like the Israelites. Don't lose your vocation like the angels. Don't lose your virtue like Sodom."

CHAPTER FIVE
Apostasy Viewed Prophetically

In the very same way, these dreamers pollute their own bodies, reject authority and slander celestial beings. But even the archangel Michael, when he was disputing with the devil about the body of Moses, did not dare to bring a slanderous accusation against him, but said, "The Lord rebuke you!" Yet these men speak abusively against whatever they do not understand; and what things they do understand by instinct, like unreasoning animals—these are the very things that destroy them. Woe to them! They have taken the way of Cain; they have rushed for profit into Balaam's error; they have been destroyed in Korah's rebellion (Jude 8-11).

I. APOSTATES POLLUTE THE WITNESS OF THE CHURCH
II. APOSTATES PERVERT THE WORSHIP OF CHRIST

In these verses the book of Jude moves from addressing apostasy in an apathetic sense to dealing with it in a prophetic sense. *Webster's New World Dictionary* defines *prophetic* as "that predicts or foreshadows." Thus, in these verses Jude is predicting what we can expect to happen during the latter days of the church age.

To me, Jude seemed to be writing about the very days in which we are living! I am becoming convinced that only a genuine spiritual awakening, a fresh wind of the Holy Spirit, can avert God's judgment on the apostasy of our nation and the world. In light of this conviction, Jude's words become extremely important to us. His purpose is to encourage the church to discern apostasy when it raises its divisive and destructive head, so that we might "earnestly contend for the faith."

Because Satan could not destroy the church from without through persecution, he is now at work to destroy it from within by means of apostasy in the pulpit and apathy in the pew. Satan is not fighting the church today; he is joining it! Jude sounded the alarm for all of us by prophesying that during the latter days apostates will follow in the way of Cain, who perverted the mode of worship; in the way of Balaam, who perverted the motive of worship; and in the way of Korah, who perverted the manner of worship. All of these marks of the apostate are not necessarily apparent in those who have "fallen away," and not all theological liberals are apostates. However it is true that those who stray from such fundamentals of our faith as the inerrancy of Scripture, the virgin birth of Christ, the vicarious death of Christ, and Christ's bodily resurrection are influenced by the spirit of apostasy, which is just as poisonous. We need many reminders if we are to stand firm in the face of apostasy.

When our daughters were little, every time they went out the front door of our home to ride their bicycles, I would say, "Do not ride your bicycles in the street!"

After each little speech would come this same reply: "We know, Daddy! How many times do you have to tell us?" Wise parents know that truths must be repeated again and again so they will sink in and become a part of their children's thoughts and actions. The same principle applies in Scripture. The Epistle of Jude is filled with much repetition. The writer has already told us in verse 5 that he wants to "remind" us of some truths even though we had known them before. Paul also practiced the repetition of important truths in his Epistles. He wrote, "Finally, my brothers, rejoice in the Lord! It is no trouble for me to write the same things to you again, and it is a safeguard for you" (Philippians 3:1).

As he viewed apostasy in a prophetic sense, Jude described some characteristics of apostates in order that we might recognize them today. While it is true that apostates may not evidence every characteristic, if they are truly apostate they will have many of the characteristics outlined in this section. Thus, Jude speaks prophetically to all of us today. His warnings are, as he said, "an example" for us during these last days.

Jude prophesied that during the last days apostates will do two things. First, they will pollute the witness of the church through immorality, insubordination, and irreverence. Second, he wrote that they will pervert the worship of Christ in mode, motive, and manner. Therefore, prophetically speaking, apostates pollute the witness of the church and pervert the worship of Christ.

I. APOSTATES POLLUTE THE WITNESS OF THE CHURCH

Apostates pollute the witness of the church with every fiber of their being—their body, soul, and spirit. In verse 8 Jude said, they "pollute their own bodies"—that is, in body, they are immoral. He continued, they "reject authority"—that is, in soul, they are insubordinate. He concluded, they "slander celestial beings" meaning, in spirit, they are irreverent.

What causes these apostates to pollute the witness of the church? Jude tells us that they are "dreamers" (Jude 8). Apostates are ignorant people who do not know about what they are speaking. They live in an unreal dream world, having accepted the lie Satan has used since the garden of Eden when he said to the woman, "You will be like God" (Genesis 3:5). As a result, Jude wrote that they "speak abusively against whatever they do not understand; and what things they do understand by instinct, like unreasoning animals—these are the very things that destroy them" (10).

In our world today, immoral actions that would have been openly rebuked in pulpits just a generation ago are accepted as "just the way it is" in many of those same pulpits today. That is because many "dreamers" in the pulpit today rock their congregants to sleep while helping them to feel comfortable in their sin. When preachers pollute their pulpits by discounting the infallibility and inerrancy of the Word of God, it is not long before their code of morals becomes polluted as well.

In Body, Apostates are Immoral.

In the words of Jude, apostates "pollute their own bodies." It is interesting that this section of verses in the Epistle begins with the phrase "in the very same way" (8). This refers us back to the sensual sins of Sodom mentioned in verse 7. The Sodomites "gave themselves up to sexual immorality." In a similar way, apostates eventually give themselves over to sensual sin. In fact, defiling the flesh is one of the first actions that follows the rejection of God's truth.

Sooner or later, most false teachers are exposed on a moral level. Jim Jones and David Koresh are prime examples of this. They were recognized by some as religious leaders, but we all know the outcome of the horrible Jonestown and Waco tragedies. On the surface these cults appeared to be filled with love, but appearances can be deceiving. Jim Jones and David Koresh defiled the flesh and, as we all know, finally destroyed it.

Remember, apostates are those who have "secretly slipped in" and turned "the grace of God into a license for immorality" (Jude 4). Only the Holy Spirit within us can stand against our fleshly desires, and the Holy Spirit is not resident in the lives of apostates.[1] We know this because Jude wrote, "These are the men who divide you, who follow mere natural instincts and do not have the Spirit" (19). We should not be surprised then that apostates pollute the witness of the church through immorality. It is no wonder they defile the flesh, because they use their liberty in Christ as a license to sin.

Apostasy and fleshly sins are genuinely linked together in Scripture. Sometimes a college student returns home saying, "I don't want to go to your church anymore. I don't believe what they teach and preach. I've learned some things at college. My professor has taught me that all of this business about God creating the heaven and earth is rubbish." Adrian Rogers astutely observes that nine out of ten times, a young person who makes statements such as this is living in sexual immorality. Apostasy and defiling the flesh are like Siamese twins.

Apostates are worse than unbelievers at this point. Peter wrote:

> If they have escaped the corruption of the world by knowing our Lord and Savior Jesus Christ and are again entangled in it and overcome, they are worse off at the end than they were at the beginning. It would have been better for them not to have known the way of righteousness, than to have known it and then to turn their backs on the sacred command that was passed on to them (2 Peter 2:20-21).

The "new morality" that we hear so much about today is nothing more than the old immorality described in the Word of God.[2] People who make light of marriage vows, live in open adultery, and join homosexual clubs and bathhouses are nothing new. Jude prophesied 1,900 years ago that one of the obvious and open marks of the age of apostasy would be that apostates "pollute their own bodies." These sensual sins of the flesh bring great dishonor to the church of the Lord Jesus Christ and pollute its witness.

When we defile the flesh, we defile our bodies, which are the temple of the Holy Spirit. We all need to be reminded that as true believers we are the dwelling place of God Himself (1 Corinthians 6:19). In the Old Testament, God had a temple for His people. But in this age of grace, He has a people for His temple. When we defile the flesh, we pollute the witness of Christ's church.

Let me emphasize a key point about sin and apostasy. Simply because a person falls into sexual sin does not mean he or she is apostate. Before any of us put on our ecclesiastical garments and look down our noses at anyone else, we should remember Paul's words: "So, if you think you are standing firm, be careful that you don't fall!" (1 Corinthians 10:12) Our Lord Himself said in the presence of a woman who was caught in defiling the flesh, "If any one of you is without sin, let him be the first to throw a stone at her" (John 8:7). Then looking into her eyes He said, "Go now and leave your life of sin."

Christ stands ready to forgive the sin of those who repent. Apostates do not seek forgiveness. They seek to justify their behavior by using the grace of God as a license for their immorality, thereby polluting the witness of the church.

In Soul, Apostates are Insubordinate

In the words of Jude, they "reject authority" (8). If the apostate is immoral in body, he or she is insubordinate in soul. Emotionally, by an act of his or her will, the apostate flat out rejects authority. Rejecting the authority that God has established is a dangerous thing. Jude's prophecy is right on target today. Doesn't our society defile the flesh and reject authority?

We should remember that the Lord Jesus said, "All authority in heaven and on earth has been given to me" (Matthew 28:18). The Greek word used here, *exousia*, means "the right" or "the authority." Thus, if Jesus has "all authority," Satan has n-o-n-e! The only authority the devil ever has over our lives is the authority we give to him. The little word *all* that Jesus used is very important: all authority originates with God. Authority in the home originates with God. Authority in the church originates with God. Authority in the workforce originates with God. Authority in government originates with God.[3] If Christ is not the authority, there is no authority.

Apostates have a real problem with authority. They seek to reject every authority that God has established, whether it be in the home, in the church, or in government. Should we be surprised that many leaders of the feminist movement believe that the Bible is a worn-out, antiquated book? After all, God Himself instituted authority in the home and the feminists reject that authority. Theological liberals who support the feminist movement neglect and reject the verses on authority in the home that are found in Ephesians 5. In fact, many of them would like to tear that passage out of the Bible.

Insubordinate apostates also reject authority in the church. Should we be surprised that leaders of dying churches and denominations are by and large men who do not uphold the inerrancy of Scripture? What we see happening today in many churches and denominations, as well as in many Christian schools, is the subtle undermining of the Bible as the infallible, inerrant, authoritative rule of faith. Jude prophesied that those possessing a spirit of apostasy will "reject authority." So we should not be surprised when the Bible—our sole authority for faith and life—is cast aside as an error-filled, antiquated book.

Apostates also reject authority in the workplace and in government. Should we be surprised that leftist regimes, which undermine governments around the world, scoff at the Bible as being totally irrelevant? It should not surprise any of us that apostate religious leaders are often associated with subversive organizations, especially in the Third World. Likewise we should not be surprised that the tremendous rise of apostasy in our nation has been accompanied by a serious and orchestrated attempt to undermine the authority of government that our forefathers established, including 150 years of Bible reading and prayer in schools.

A rejection of the Bible's authority goes hand in hand with a demand for a new social order.

Apostates reject authority because in reality they reject the Lord Jesus Christ and His rule over their lives. Apostates do not want a God who rules over them. Their battle cry is, "Freedom!" They don't want to be boxed in by any parameters. Having fallen away from the faith, they take the precious Biblical doctrine of the priesthood of believers, and pervert it by making it a license to believe anything they wish to believe.

As Christians we believe in religious liberty and freedom, but we also believe in personal responsibility. If professors in our schools and colleges do not believe in the fundamentals of Biblical faith, they need to say so instead of hiding behind theological double-talk. No one should be coerced into believing anything, but we who are custodians of the faith have the responsibility to "contend for the faith." We should not have to pay for the propagation of liberal poison in our schools and denominations that, under the guise of freedom and priesthood, denies the inerrancy of Scripture.

Currently, liberal voices in much of the secular press say that the great danger facing America today comes from fundamentalist Christians who are faithful to the Word of God and believe it in a literal sense. Nothing could be further from the truth. The greatest danger comes from liberal theologians and apostates who "reject authority." These apostates pollute the witness of the church in body by being immoral, and in soul by being insubordinate.

In Spirit, Apostates are Irreverent

In the words of Jude, they "slander celestial beings" (8). Apostates who fall away from the faith and become immoral in body and insubordinate in soul also are irreverent in spirit. The Greek word rendered "celestial beings" in this verse is *doxa,* which literally means "glorious ones." Apostates are irreverent in spirit toward the things of God. They pollute the witness of the church by cynicism, ridicule, and blasphemy. The phrase "speak evil," (KJV) which is repeated in verse 10, literally means "to blaspheme." Jude was not just writing about taking the Lord's name in vain when he used the phrase "slander celestial beings." He is also writing about apostates who take God's Word lightly, deliberately joke about it and make light of His created beings.

The apostle John, exiled to Patmos as an old man, addressed the pastors of the seven churches of Asia in the book of Revelation by referring to them as "angels" (Revelation 2–3). Therefore, *The Century Bible* suggests that the phrase "speak evil of dignitaries" (KJV) found in Jude 8 refers to the "constituted authorities of the church." In other words, Jude is saying that apostates speak evil of God's appointed and anointed leadership.

From where does this spirit of cynicism and accusation come? It comes from Satan, for we remember that the Bible refers to Satan as the "accuser of our brothers" (Revelation 12:10). Christians fall into Satan's trap and do his work every time they "speak evil" of each other, especially of those whom God has placed in positions of authority.

Jude cited an example of Michael, the archangel, in order to illustrate the danger of speaking unnecessary evil concerning one whom God has placed in authority. He wrote, "But even the archangel Michael, when he was disputing with the devil about the body of Moses, did not dare to bring a slanderous accusation against him, but said, 'The Lord rebuke you!'" (Jude 9)

This passage is interesting in that there is no other information in the Bible concerning the struggle between Satan and Michael for the body of Moses that could throw light on its cause or consequence. However we do know that "Moses the servant of the Lord died there in Moab, as the Lord had said. He buried him in Moab in the valley opposite Beth Peor; but to this day no one knows where his grave is" (Deuteronomy 34:5-6). Commentators speculate on all sorts of scenarios concerning this episode. All we know is that Moses died prematurely on Mount Nebo. No one knows where he is buried.

This passage becomes significant when we realize that Satan has always tried to pollute and pervert the true worship of our Lord. He has filled the world with counterfeits. He has deceived millions by getting them to focus their worship on relics such as bones, shrouds, or the like. In so doing he causes people to take the focus of worship off the Lord and place it on some relic.

This truth was brought home to me when my wife and I visited the garden tomb in Jerusalem. While there we conversed with a

Britisher. As we discussed the validity of the site, with a thick English brogue he said, "It's not the cocoon we look at and talk about; it is the butterfly!" How true! We do not worship the tomb of Christ or any other relic. We worship the butterfly, the risen Christ! However, Satan knew the history of the children of Israel and how prone they were to worship relics. He was convinced that if he could get the body of Moses, he could make the people worship the relic instead of the Lord!

Jude obviously included this verse in his Epistle for a reason because "every word of God is flawless" (Proverbs 30:5). I believe the point is that Michael the archangel did not rebuke Satan but left the matter to the Lord, saying, "The Lord rebuke you!" If the archangel is careful in how he deals with Satan, how much more careful should we be? As mighty as Michael is, he has more respect for the devil than some human beings have for Almighty God and His holy creation! If Michael, who represented a good cause, spoke courteously to Satan, how heinous it is for ungodly people who represent an evil cause to speak irreverently of the authority of God and His church!

Apostates pollute the witness of the church in body, in soul, and in spirit. They are immoral, insubordinate, and irreverent because they are ignorant! Jude wrote that they simply do not know anything about which they are speaking. In fact, they act and reason like animals: They "speak abusively against whatever they do not understand; and what things they do understand by instinct, like unreasoning animals—these are the very things that destroy them" (Jude 10). Apostates live solely by natural instinct, just like animals. There is nothing spiritual about them. Professing to be wise, they have become fools.

What is the outcome of apostates who pollute the witness of the church? Through their immorality, insubordination, and irreverence, apostates corrupt and destroy themselves. They criticize everything that they do not understand and destroy themselves in the process.[4] That is the prophetic tragedy of it all. When people play with fire, they get burned. God has not abdicated His throne; He is still in charge!

It is important to remember that Jude's words were written about apostates who have knowledge of God's truth but not life, not about atheists or authentic believers. We are not surprised when atheists and apostates speak evil about the truths of God. But what a warning this is for any authentic believer who is tempted to "slander celestial beings." God forbid!

Looking around us today, we may wonder if the complete fulfillment of Jude's prophesy is near. Never before have we heard so many people maligning God's appointed leadership. Moses' authorship of the Pentateuch is openly scoffed at, even though the Lord Jesus affirmed it when "beginning with Moses and all the Prophets, he explained to them what was said in all the Scriptures concerning himself" (Luke 24:27). We are living in a theological environment in which people and institutions that truly adhere to the inerrancy of Scripture are attacked and accused of all manner of evil. We see apostasy revealing itself in a prophetic sense before our eyes.

So what is the church to do? In the words of David, "When the foundations are being destroyed, what can the righteous do?" (Psalm 11:3) We are to "contend for the faith that was once for all entrusted to the saints" by loving the faith, learning the faith, living the faith, and loosing the faith!

II. Apostates Pervert the Worship of Christ

In Jude 11 God pronounced a "woe" on those who are guilty of apostasy. This is a serious matter. The word "woe" is used in the Greek language to note a culmination or a calamity, to communicate hopelessness and sorrow. Kenneth Wuest, in his volume on the Greek New Testament, points out, "woe is an interjection of enunciation." Woe is pronounced on three types of apostate individuals: those who pervert the worship of Christ in mode (Cain), motive (Balaam), and manner (Korah). This serious sentence of woe is irrevocable and final.

Why has Jude told us about the ruin of Cain, Balaam, and Korah? I believe he wanted us to avoid their misery. Those of us who open the Book of God to the people of God should warn of coming judgment as well as speak sweet promises of the good news of the Gospel. Therefore we must warn people from all walks of life about the dangers of apostasy. Apostasy is not confined to one class of people. Cain was a farmer. Balaam was a prophet. Korah was a priest. In the words of Maxwell Coder, "There are apostates in the pulpit, in the palace, and in the poorhouse!"

Apostates Pervert the Mode of Worship

In the words of Jude, they "have taken the way of Cain" (11). What is "the way of Cain"? The answer is found in Genesis 4:1-7, the account of one of the first worship services in human history:

> Adam lay with his wife Eve, and she became pregnant and gave birth to Cain. She said, "With the help of the Lord I have brought forth a man." Later she gave birth to his brother Abel. Now Abel kept flocks, and Cain worked the soil. In the course of time Cain brought some of the fruits of the soil as an offering to the Lord. But Abel brought fat portions from some of the firstborn of his flock. The Lord looked with favor on Abel and his offering, but on Cain and his offering he did not look with favor. So Cain was very angry, and his face was downcast. Then the Lord said to Cain, "Why are you angry? Why is your face downcast? If you do what is right, will you not be accepted? But if you do not do what is right, sin is crouching at your door; it desires to have you, but you must master it."

Abel brought a sacrificial offering from his flock and shed the blood as an offering to God. Why did God respect his offering? God was teaching us all a lesson that "without the shedding of blood there is no forgiveness [of sin]" (Hebrews 9:22). Sin has never been forgiven without the shedding of blood. That is why 1 John 1:7 reads, "the blood of Jesus, his [God's] Son, purifies us from all sin." Abel's lamb was a picture of the blood of Christ on the cross of Calvary.

Cain, on the other hand, brought an offering of the works of his hands. No doubt he brought the ripest grain and the best of his crop, but God would not accept it! One may be prone to think that this seems unfair. After all, Cain was a good, hard-working man. We are prone to think that since he did his best, God should accept his actions! That is the reasoning of those who pervert the mode of worship by taking "the way of Cain." They express it this way today:

"Why, Joe is good, hard-working, and isn't lazy. He is kind to others. God should accept him into Heaven." Many preachers preach this message of good works and perhaps some of my readers reason in this way. The way of Abel however is the way of faith. The way of Cain is the way of works—a religion without faith that is based primarily on good works.

Cain was the first apostate. He knew the only way to approach God, to worship, was through the blood of the sacrifice by faith. Yet he attempted to approach God through the work of his hands, without the blood of an innocent substitute. In so doing, he perverted the mode of worship.

Abel's gift, on the other hand, was brought by faith. Faith is believing what God says. The Bible says, "By faith Abel offered God a better sacrifice than Cain did. By faith he was commended as a righteous man, when God spoke well of his offerings. And by faith he still speaks, even though he is dead" (Hebrews 11:4).

Cain however set aside the word of God. There is little doubt that he had heard, upon his parents' knees, of the folly of trying to cover up his sins by himself. Adam and Eve had learned this lesson the hard way. After they fell into sin, they sought to cover their sin with the leaves of a fig tree but quickly found out that fig leaves would not suffice. Cain had heard how God had provided a substitutionary covering when He slew an innocent animal and used the skins to provide a covering for his parents. Even knowing this, he chose to go his own way.

Cain rejected the way of substitutionary atonement and, too proud to admit his need of a substitute, offered the best of his own efforts. We all need to be reminded that the Bible says, "For it is by grace you have been saved, through faith—and this not from yourselves, it is the gift of God—not by works, so that no one can boast" (Ephesians 2:8-9). The substitutionary sacrifice commanded of Cain prefigured the vicarious atonement made by Christ at Calvary. Cain rejected God's divinely appointed way to Christ—by faith through His shed blood. Sadly, the Bible records, "Cain went out from the Lord's presence" (Genesis 4:16). This is still the plight of people today who pervert the mode of worship and go the way of Cain. They too go out from the presence of the Lord for all eternity.

One sure characteristic of an apostate is his lack of emphasis on the vicarious death of our Lord Jesus Christ and His shed blood as an atonement for our sin. The apostate who does not teach or preach on the blood of Christ has gone the way of Cain. One would say, "Surely this perversion of the mode of worship is not taught by professors in Christian schools!" Yet, with a broken heart, I have to tell you that some seminary professors today teach young preachers that vicarious punishment is not meaningful or moral. Some even suggest that it is unwise to emphasize our need for the cross of Christ. This is going the way of Cain and setting aside the necessity of the blood atonement.

Let's call an Old Testament witness to testify concerning this matter. Let's ask Isaiah what he thinks about the blood atonement and the substitutionary death of Christ. Hear his reply:

> But he was pierced for our transgressions, he was crushed for our iniquities; the punishment that brought us peace was upon him, and by his wounds we are healed. We all, like sheep, have gone astray, each of us has turned to his own way; and the Lord has laid on him the iniquity of us all (Isaiah 53:5-6).

Let's also call a New Testament witness, the apostle Paul, to see what he says concerning the substitutionary death of Christ. He replies, "For what I received I passed on to you as of first importance: that Christ died for our sins according to the Scriptures" (1 Corinthians 15:3). Thank God for the vicarious, substitutionary death of the Lord Jesus Christ on the cross. May God have mercy on those who discount it.

What should we do today when so many pervert the worship of Christ by going "the way of Cain"? We need all the more to "contend for the faith." People accuse conservatives of having a lust for power in our schools today when they simply long for Biblical purity. I am not suggesting by any stretch of the imagination that all liberals are apostates. Most of them are not. But I am saying that anyone who discounts the absolute necessity of the cross and the blood atonement is obviously influenced by the spirit of apostasy.

There are only two religions in the world: true religion and false religion. True religion is represented by Abel and the blood sacrifice; false religion is represented by Cain and all the others who try to get to Heaven by their own good works.

It is amazing how many people who regularly attend church every Sunday are "going the way of Cain." In so doing they pervert the worship of Christ through their mode of worship. The way of Cain leads headlong into Hell, whereas the way of the cross leads to Heaven. In many churches across our land, people sit week after week, month after month, year after year, and never hear a message on the blood of Christ or the fact that Christ died as a substitute for our sins.

Solomon spoke of "the way of Cain" when he said, "There is a way that seems right to a man, but in the end it leads to death" (Proverbs 16:25). Millions of people in America today are members of Cain's church. Their name is on the roll of churches where Christ's blood is never mentioned and where the theology of "being good" is believed to be enough to get to Heaven. They, in turn, are rearing a generation of children who know nothing about the necessity or urgency of the cross. For them, it is simply a sentimental story. Some denominations have gone so far as to omit songs about the blood of Christ in their hymnals. We would all do well to remember the words of Charles Hadden Spurgeon, the prince of preachers: "The true test of whether a man is preaching the Gospel or not is the emphasis he places on the blood of Christ." Every church member should ask this question: "When was the last time I heard a sermon on the blood of Christ and the necessity of the cross?"

When the Biblical truth of the necessity of Christ's shed blood is replaced with some other message, the preacher has gone the way of Cain. One of the subtle dangers of today's "positive" preaching is that the blood is seldom, if ever, mentioned. We are told that we are the greatest, that there is good in all of us by nature. We are told that we can do anything if we simply set our minds to it. This is the way of Cain, who said in essence, "I'll do it, and I'll do it my way." All the positive thinking in the world could not make Cain's offering acceptable to God. For the same reason, all the positive thinking in the world cannot negate the cross of Christ.

A century ago, General William Booth—founder of the Salvation Army—said that the chief danger of the twentieth century would be "religion without Christ, salvation without regeneration, politics without God, and Heaven without Hell." Jude also prophesied that the way of Cain would be prevalent during the last days of the church age. Today we see that the prophecies of Jude and General

Booth were absolutely correct. We live in a day where there is religion without Christ, salvation without regeneration, politics without God, and Heaven without Hell.

People who go the way of Cain are too proud to admit that they are sinners and need Christ's substitutionary sacrifice. In turn, they may willingly give the best of their efforts to God. Many church goers, if asked to do something hard, would be the first in line to say, "Let me do it." If they believed they would have to do something hard in order to be saved, they would do it. If they were asked to give a big gift, they would give it. If they were asked to work on some project, they would roll up their sleeves and present the best their hands could do. But when asked to humble themselves and admit their need of a substitutionary Savior who died for their sins, they are too proud to accept that! Such is the way of Cain that perverts the mode of worship.

The followers of Cain tell us that the way of this new age is the way of humanism. They tell us that man is all sufficient and that all he needs to do is the best he can. They say that people need no substitutionary atonement. But if any of us get the idea that the way of Cain will get us to Heaven, we had best remember the words of Jessie B. Pounds:

> I must needs go home by the way of the cross,
> There's no other way but this;
> I shall ne'er get sight of the gates of light,
> If the way of the cross I miss.
>
> I must needs go on in the blood-sprinkled way,
> The path that the Savior trod,
> If I ever climb to the heights sublime,
> Where the soul is at home with God.
>
> The way of the cross leads home,
> The way of the cross leads home,
> It is sweet to know as I onward go
> The way of the cross leads home.

What is your mode of worship? Is it the way of Abel? Do you trust in the substitutionary atonement of the shed blood of Christ for your salvation? Or, do you go in the direction of Cain, trying to get to Heaven by being good and presenting the best of your own works? The world tells us that the way to Heaven is through the religion of humanism or our own good works. So, like Cain, many people bring gifts that are not acceptable to God. The prophetic tragedy of it all is that God says, "Yet these men speak abusively against whatever they do not understand; and what things they do understand by instinct, like unreasoning animals, these are the very things that destroy them" (Jude 10). God says, in effect, "Woe to them who pursue the way of Cain."

Apostates Pervert the Motive of Worship

Our motive for worshiping should be to meet God and glorify Him. However, apostates pervert the motive of worship by rushing "for profit into Balaam's error" (Jude 11). What does this phrase mean? What is the error of Balaam? His story is found in Numbers 22–24.

King Balak of Moab was afraid and intimidated by the Israelites, who had camped in the plains of Moab near the Jordan river across from Jericho. So he decided to bribe the gentile prophet Balaam with a set fee in order to persuade Balaam to curse the Israelites. Balaam refused and sent the King's messengers away. However the more he thought about it the greedier his heart became. To make a long story short, Balaam returned to Balak and said in effect, "I cannot curse them but I have a plan which will cause God to curse them for you (for a fee of course!)" So Balaam arranged for some seductive Moabite women to invite Israelite men to a big sensual feast. It was not long before fornication took over and the curse of God came upon His people, resulting in the tragic judgment and death of twenty-four thousand Israelites! (See Numbers 25:1-9 and 31:15-16.)

The error of Balaam was in using his spiritual insight to obtain material gain. His error was not just in doing what he did but in thinking that he could get away with it. Balaam was involved in religion for what he could gain from it. We read in 2 Peter 2:15 that Balaam "loved the wages of wickedness." Whereas Cain perverted the mode of worship, Balaam perverted the motive of worship. This is clearly revealed to us in Jude 11, where we note that Balaam's action was "for profit."

Balaam genuinely sought to please God, but he sought to please men and himself at the same time. Focusing on this point our Lord said, "No one can serve two masters. Either he will hate the one and love the other, or he will be devoted to the one and despise the other. You cannot serve God and Money" (Matthew 6:24).

Peter addressed this issue of the true motive of worship as well:

> But there were also false prophets among the people, just as there will be false teachers among you. They will secretly introduce destructive heresies, even denying the sovereign Lord who bought them—bringing swift destruction on themselves. Many will follow their shameful ways and will bring the way of truth into disrepute. In their greed these teachers will exploit you with stories they have made up. Their condemnation has long been hanging over them, and their destruction has not been sleeping (2 Peter 2:1-3).

Apostates are filled with covetousness and are generally motivated by money. Paul said they are "lovers of pleasure rather than lovers of God" (2 Timothy 3:4).

Each of us should ask ourselves a personal question: "What is our motive for worshiping Christ?" Is our motive to obtain what we can get out of it? Or is our motive to glorify God? Some people join certain churches in order to make business contacts. There is nothing wrong with Christians doing business with each other—as long as their motives are pure. But woe be unto those who pervert the motive of worship by rushing "for profit into Balaam's error."

The tragedy of Balaam is that he stifled his convictions to obtain temporary gain. Some people today also alter their message in the spirit of covetousness. The preacher who yields to such temptations, for example, does so in the spirit of Balaam and is guilty of compromise. Anyone, anywhere, who alters the Word of God for advantage or gain has the spirit of apostasy. The prophetic tragedy is that Jude says this will happen. He also makes it clear that God places His irrevocable "woe" upon such apostate actions. Our sole motive should be to glorify the Lord!

Apostates Pervert the Manner Of Worship

According to Jude, "they have been destroyed in Korah's rebellion." True worship does everything decently and in order. Paul wrote, "Do nothing out of selfish ambition or vain conceit, but in humility consider others better than yourselves" (Philippians 2:3). He also wrote that believers are to submit to one another out of reverence for Christ (Ephesians 5:21). But Korah perverted the manner of worship because he had a real problem with authority.

The word "rebellion" in verse 11 comes from the Greek word *antilogia,* which literally means "against the word."[5] Cain ignored the word of God, Balaam opposed the word of God, and Korah rebelled against the word of God. This is the progression of the apostate. He begins by simply ignoring what the Bible says then progresses into opposing the Bible by trying to say that it is not the Word of God but simply contains the word of God. Once the apostate reaches this point, it is not long before he, like Korah, openly rebels against God and His holy Word.

The story of Korah is found in Numbers 16. Korah was a Levite who, lured by pride, formed a conspiracy with three other men and led two hundred of Israel's elders in a rebellion against Moses (God's prophet) and Aaron (God's priest). Moses and Aaron were appointed by God, and Korah was too blind to see that by opposing them, he opposed God. He did not want to submit to Moses' leadership and authority. Remember, Jude wrote that they "reject authority" (Jude 8), so every apostate is a rebel at heart!

Apostates pervert the manner of worship by being divisive and by bringing dissension into the church. They forget that God said, "Do not touch my anointed ones; do my prophets no harm" (1 Chronicles 16:22). They also forget that God has warned, "I will contend with those who contend with you" (Isaiah 49:25).

When Moses heard of the rebels' accusations and their under-cutting of his position of authority, he "fell facedown" (Numbers 16:4). Moses did not take their actions personally. He did not take it out on the people. He took the problem to the Lord! He saw right through their wicked hearts to the real issue of jealousy. He left the issue in God's hands because he knew that in reality they were opposing God, and not him. Moses was simply the closest person to God with whom they could identify.

What did the Lord do? Numbers 16:31-35 reveals:

As soon as he [Moses] finished saying all this, the ground under them split apart and the earth opened its mouth and swallowed them, with their households and all Korah's men and all their possessions. They went down alive into the grave, with everything they owned; the earth closed over them, and they perished and were gone from the community. At their cries, all the Israelites around them fled, shouting, "The earth is going to swallow us too!" And fire came out from the Lord and consumed the 250 men who were offering the incense.

God has His own ways of vindicating the holiness of His name. The Bible simply says, "they perished." God does not severely punish all apostates and all who have a spirit of apostasy while they live on earth. He does not strike dead everyone who lies today, as He did to Ananias and Sapphira in the book of Acts. In these instances He set an example that all of us should heed.

God commands His appointed undershepherds of the flock to do two things: to lead the flock and to feed the flock. Sad to say, some pastors neither lead nor feed the church of God today. Personally, I believe that if a church has a pastor who doesn't lead and feed the people, they ought to find another undershepherd. Other pastors want to lead their flocks in a dictatorial way without ever feeding them. Still others want to feed the flock until they are fat, but do not take the responsibility and the risk of leading them to new spiritual heights. There is a great need today for God-appointed and God-anointed pastors who love the people, who are fearless and faithful, and who will lead the flock, not just feed it. Many churches are dying simply because they lack strong spiritual leadership.

Conversely, it is also true that some godly pastors who lead and feed the flock are opposed and undercut by the spirit of apostasy, as manifested in the rebellion of Korah. Men and women in some churches refuse to be under authority. Like Korah, they gather groups about them to oppose God's anointed and appointed. Heaven only knows how many churches have split because of the same spirit of apostasy that caused men and women to perish during the rebellion of Korah. Korah did not want his God-appointed pastor, Moses, to feed him or lead him, so he rebelled against Moses' authority. But God contended with Korah because His Word is true: "I'll contend with those who contend with you."

The warning here is that when we speak unjustly against God's appointed and anointed, we speak against the Lord Himself, who bestows all authority. Paul sounded this warning in his Epistle to Titus: "Remind the people to be subject to rulers and authorities, to be obedient, to be ready to do whatever is good, to slander no one, to be peaceable and considerate, and to show true humility toward all men" (Titus 3:1-2).

The experience of Korah is recorded for all posterity as an example of a man who, in his own quest for power and recognition, defied God's legitimate authority over the people of God. There are those in churches today who seek to undermine the authority of the church. These present-day apostates speak evil of God and His appointed and anointed. They, like Diotrophes, "love the preeminent place." That is one reason why some churches never receive the blessing and glory of God.

As we note the progression of Jude 11, we see a vivid picture of the apostate's plight. Note the tense of the verbs: "have taken...have rushed...have been destroyed." The apostate goes down the wrong road and before long finds himself running down that road until he finally crashes. Apostasy moves at an ever-increasing speed, always downhill.

One of the prophetic tragedies found in the book of Jude is that there is no hope for the apostate. God shows us in these verses what He thinks of apostasy. He pronounces "woe" upon apostates. Is it any wonder that Jude sounds a warning to any and all who pervert the worship of Christ in mode, motive, or manner? We would be wise to consider our manner of worship, whether we lift ourselves up by tearing others down. May God grant us wisdom to discern false prophets who pollute the witness of the church and pervert the worship of Christ. Consider too what happens when a person takes a strong stand for holiness and contends earnestly for the faith. Often that person will be called narrow-minded, mean, and power-hungry by the apostate world today. May God give us grace and courage to "contend earnestly for the faith."

Jude's prophetic look at apostasy is coming true today all around us. Apostates are polluting the witness of the church in body, soul, and spirit. They are immoral, insubordinate, and irreverent. They also pervert the worship of Christ. They go the way of Cain and pervert the mode of worship. They run greedily in the error of Balaam and pervert the motive of worship. They follow in the rebellion of Korah and pervert the manner of worship. It is as though Jude were alive today and writing to us through the morning newspaper.

Jude's prophetic warning should cause each of us to ask ourselves two questions: "Is my witness polluted or clean? Is my worship of Christ perverted or clear?"

The danger of apostasy is to know the will of God and not to act on it. We all need to learn from the illustrations of the three men mentioned in Jude 11. Fearful judgment awaits those who, like Cain, know Gods truth and reject it. May what was said of Cain not be said of any of us: "[he] went out from the presence of the Lord." What haunting words!

Since apostates pollute the witness of the church and pervert the worship of Christ, what is the church to do? Or, as David asked, "When the foundations are being destroyed, What can the righteous do?" I repeat, we are to "contend for the faith that was once for all entrusted to the saints." If not now, when? True believers who keep silent and make faith-related compromises to avoid conflict and confrontation will be held responsible.

CHAPTER SIX
Apostasy Viewed Cosmetically

These men are blemishes at your love feasts, eating with you without the slightest qualm—shepherds who feed only themselves. They are clouds without rain, blown along by the wind; autumn trees, without fruit and uprooted—twice dead. They are wild waves of the sea, foaming up their shame; wandering stars, for whom blackest darkness has been reserved forever. Enoch, the seventh from Adam, prophesied about these men: "See, the Lord is coming with thousands upon thousands of his holy ones to judge everyone, and to convict all the ungodly of all the ungodly acts they have done in the ungodly way, and of all the harsh words ungodly sinners have spoken against him." These men are grumblers and faultfinders; they follow their own evil desires; they boast about themselves and flatter others for their own advantage (Jude 12-16).

I. APOSTATES ARE EASILY DETECTED
II. APOSTATES ARE ETERNALLY DOOMED

A newspaper carried a story about a local bank robbery. The article was accompanied by a photograph, taken by the bank's security camera, of the robber standing at the teller's booth. He was dressed in a full disguise that included a hat, glasses, and an obviously false mustache. Cosmetically, he had changed his appearance in order to hide his real identity.

The article reminded me of the warning Jude gave us that spiritual criminals, who are cosmetically disguised, seek to rob the church of power and blessing. He described them for us in order that we might know what they look like. In a first-century way he splashed their pictures across the book that bears his name in order to show us that apostates are cosmetic Christians who pretend to be something they are not.

The word "cosmetic" is derived from the Greek word *kosmetikos,* which means "skilled in decorating or covering over; it is to dress up something in order to give it an appearance on the surface that is unlike its reality." Claiming to be true believers, apostates are only cosmetic believers. They are not the real thing. They know the truth of Christ and may even embrace it intellectually for a while, but they turn from it. They are "into" religion and know nothing about a relationship with Christ. Apostates disguise themselves to look like authentic believers, infiltrate the church, and in so doing bring confusion and conflict.

Cosmetic Christians are all around us. They are in our churches, schools, and denominations. Jude reveals however that those whose faith and fellowship are merely cosmetic are easily detected and eternally doomed.

I. Apostates Are Easily Detected

Although it is true that apostates "secretly slipped in," it is also true that if we take time to discern, they are easily detected. In verses 12-13 Jude used five metaphors to illustrate how these irreverent impostors give themselves away. He said they are like hidden spots (rocks), that reveal their lack of peace. They are like waterless clouds that reveal their lack of productivity. They are like fruitless trees that reveal their lack of proof. They are like raging waves that bring the filth of the ocean to the shore and reveal their lack of purity. They are like wandering stars that reveal their lack of purpose.

Apostates Lack Peace

Apostates—cosmetic Christians—are, in the words of Jude, like "blemishes [hidden rocks] at your love feasts." The margin notes in most Bibles reveal that the Greek word translated "blemishes" literally means "hidden rocks or sunken reefs." It provides the picture of large rocks just below the water's surface. These rocks cannot be seen by the naked eye until it is too late. Cosmetic Christians are unseen dangers. They tear up church fellowship and destroy its love. Satan planted cosmetic Christians like hidden rocks in the love feasts of the New Testament church in order to cause division and dissension. The tragedy of the early church was that the believers did not recognize these impostors until they had destroyed their fellowship.

Sooner or later, many of us who live near the water have had the experience of being on a boat that runs aground. As we were skimming along the surface of the water, perhaps the boat suddenly lurched, came to a stop, and began to leak. We quickly discovered that a rock hidden beneath the surface had done all the damage.

It is interesting that Jude compared these cosmetic Christians to hidden rocks located "in our love feasts." Tertullian, in his defense of Christianity before the Roman government in A.D. 197, described these love feasts. He, as well as early church historians recorded that during the early days of the church, Christians gathered weekly for the love feasts, which amounted to large fellowship meals where everyone present shared food, fun, and fellowship. The rich and poor, the young and old, gathered for these happy occasions.[1]

However the early church ceased having these love feasts because apostates infiltrated the church and turned the love feasts into cliques that furthered their selfish ambitions. They came, in the words of Jude, to "feed only themselves." In some cases the feasts even degenerated into drunken orgies. Paul plainly revealed that the love feast at the church in Corinth had degenerated into shameful drunkenness and immorality. In fact, he rebuked the Corinthian Christians severely in 1 Corinthians.

In navigating his ship at sea, a captain is not concerned with the reefs and rocks that are clearly marked on the charts. It is the uncharted reef or rock that is hidden just below the surface that brings the greatest danger.[2] The same danger is present in the church. Cosmetic Christians are hidden in our love feasts. They may appear to be safe and calm, but as Jude says, they are nothing more than "hidden reefs."

How many churches today, while sailing across the ocean of love and fellowship, have run aground because cosmetic Christians, like hidden rocks and sunken reefs, have brought discord and dissension? False doctrines and selfish motives that lie just below the surface pose hidden dangers. The devil obviously desires to bring discord and dissension to the church because no one wants to be a part of a fellowship in which fussing and fighting are prevalent. That is why people are seldom saved in churches that do not manifest a sweet fellowship. I am convinced that the most important factor in church growth is love and unity among the fellowship of believers. Wise pastors steer their churches around hidden reefs.

Cosmetic Christians are easily detected because they lack peace. They are peace-breakers, not peacemakers. Our Lord said, "Blessed are the peacemakers, for they will be called sons of God" (Matthew 5:9). He pronounced a blessing on the peacemakers, not the peace-lovers. He blessed those who promote unity. Notice that He did not say that the peacemakers would be "made" the sons of God. He said that they will be "called" the sons of God. That is, they will be recognized as committed Christians. Cosmetic Christians however have no peace about them. That is why Jude says they are easily detected.

Apostates Lack Productivity

In Jude's words, apostates "are clouds without rain, blown along by the wind" (12). By using the metaphor of clouds, Jude wanted us to know that apostates—cosmetic Christians—are easily detected not only by a lack of peace but by a lack of productivity. Like clouds without water, they are filled with empty promises.

Nothing can be as despairing to a farmer than to see clouds that bring no water during times of drought. My first pastorate was in Hobart, Oklahoma, a wheat farming center of the world. The wheat harvest in southwestern Oklahoma takes place around June 1 each year. It is, of course, dependent on ample spring rains. The entire livelihood of most of those faithful farmers depends on that June harvest. I well remember one particular year of drought. No rain had fallen for weeks and weeks. The outlook was bleak. Crops were shriveling up. Everything that should have been green was brown. Flowers faded. Livestock suffered. Tanks and reservoirs ran dry. One day around noon clouds began to roll in from the south, and the whole town went into a frenzy! People even gathered on the courthouse lawn to welcome the coming rain. But a strange and disappointing thing happened. The clouds, which had not been seen for months, just sailed by without depositing a drop. Filled with promise, they did not deliver. They left a bunch of faithful farmers with nothing but deep disappointment.

Jude wrote that cosmetic Christians, like rainless clouds, are easily detected by their lack of productivity. They have the right appearance, but possess nothing of substance. They may talk a good game, but their productivity is nil. For example, they even stand in pulpits every Sunday but produce nothing. People sit in some churches week after week, listening to "clouds-without-water" pastors while they thirst for the water of life. They hear words without wonders and promises without productivity.

Why is this? Many men in the pulpit look the way they ought to look, say the right things, but never produce. They may have great ability but they only produce empty promises as they "boast about themselves and, flatter others for their own advantage" (Jude 16). They promote all the latest denominational programs and catchy slogans. They are filled with promises and new ideas for bigger and better days ahead. But mostly it is just talk. There is little productivity. In our own denomination, it breaks my heart that in any given year one out of four pastors does not lead anyone to Christ. Sadly, eight thousand churches baptize one or fewer people per church every year. There is little fruit, just "clouds without rain."

Apostates appear to have much potential and personality, but all the while the refreshing rain never falls. They are quick to boast of their abilities, but they never produce spiritual fruit. Solomon said, "Like clouds and wind without rain is a man who boasts of gifts he does not give" (Proverbs 25:14). Apostates survive by knowing the right people in the right places, but when all is said and done they are sadly like "clouds without rain." They lack productivity.

Apostates Lack Proof

Jude wrote that cosmetic Christians, who are easily detected by a lack of peace and productivity, are also easily detected by a lack of proof. They are "autumn trees, without fruit and uprooted—twice dead" (12). What does Jude mean by this metaphor?

In the Middle East, the harvest falls well before late autumn, the season when trees shed their leaves. Late autumn is not a season when fruit would be expected. Thus the picture Jude describes is one of late autumn trees whose branches are bare and leafless as winter approaches.[3] These trees are "without fruit." They are void of life-giving sap. They are sterile.

The only way a branch can bring forth fruit is by receiving life from the vine or trunk. Cosmetic Christians cannot produce fruit because the fruit of the Spirit is the by-product of the life of Christ within. They have never been attached to the vine by the new birth. They do not have the life of Christ—the Spirit—within them (19), therefore they have no fruit. Lacking the ability to produce fruit, they cannot build up schools or churches so they attach themselves like leeches to Christian schools and churches that have been built on the life-giving, infallible truth of the Word of God and begin to suck the spiritual life out of them. Apostates have no power in and of themselves. They are like clouds without water and trees without fruit.

Liberal theology cannot produce fruit! It has never built a great Christian school, although it has sucked the spiritual life out of many. It has never founded and built a great church, although it has sucked the spiritual life out of many.

Jude next revealed that apostates are not only like late autumn trees without fruit, but that they are "twice dead." He wrote that they have been "uprooted." Maxwell Coder said, "They have no fruit of profession because they have no root of possession."[4] Many trees appear to be dead during late autumn, but those possessing life will bloom again. However, apostates who are twice dead appear to be spiritually dead because they are spiritually dead. They do not produce spiritual fruit. They are sterile and lifeless. No matter how often the apostate says he believes the Bible, his seed is not producing fruit in his personal life and ministry. Why? Because such a person has no spiritual root! Jude 19 plainly says the apostate does not have the Spirit.

What do we do with dead trees? We can prune them, but that will not give them life. We can transplant and cultivate them, but if they are dead they will not come to life again. So Jude wrote that these trees—apostates—are "up-rooted." That is, they are torn up by the roots and disposed by burning. John the Baptist referred to this when he said, "The axe is already at the root of the trees, and every tree that does not produce good fruit will be cut down and thrown into the fire" (Matthew 3:10). Jesus also said, "If anyone does not remain in me, he is like a branch that is thrown away and withers; such branches are picked up, thrown into the fire and burned" (John 15:6).

Apostates are "autumn trees without fruit and uprooted—twice dead." The first death is spiritual death; the second death is the lake of fire. If we are born once, we will die twice; if we are born twice, we will only die once. Cosmetic Christians are twice dead because they have only been born once. They have never been born again by the Spirit of God.

What is the proof of the Christian life? Jesus said in the sermon on the mount, "By their fruit you will recognize them" (Matthew 7:16). The fruit is the proof, one of the obvious evidences of authentic salvation. The Lord Jesus told the parable of the sower to show us that the seed that falls on the hard ground, the shallow ground, or the thorny ground brings forth no fruit. The only seed that brings forth fruit is that which is planted in the good ground and is rooted in Christ.

The seed that brings forth fruit is also the seed that glorifies the Father. Jesus said, "This is to my Father's glory that you bear much fruit showing yourselves to be my disciples" (John 15:8). Jesus also revealed that His Father is the gardener: "I am the true vine, and my Father is the gardener" (John 15:1). When a branch bears fruit, it bears witness to the gardener's skill and care. Men judge the worth of the gardener by the fruit of his garden.

Cosmetic Christians have nothing to give and nothing to show. They are like trees without fruit. Not only are they fruitless, they are rootless.

Apostates Lack Purity

In Jude's words, apostates are "wild waves of the sea, foaming up their shame" (13). By this metaphor Jude means that apostates expose themselves. They are like wild waves that leave the filth and shame of their innermost being on the shores of life for all to see. Cosmetic Christians are easily detected by a lack of purity.

People who live by the ocean and observe it every day can learn a lot about it. When the weather is calm, the ocean is crystal clear. But when storms come and winds of the hurricane season blow, the ocean begins to churn. Raging waves bring up the filth and debris from the ocean floor and deposit it with its foam on the shore. After each storm, the shore is always dotted with beach-combers who find all sorts of things, ranging from rotting, dead fish to shining shells that had been resting on the ocean floor.

Cosmetic Christians are just like the ocean's raging waves. They are easily detected by lack of purity. They may, for example, lose their tempers when a storm comes and in a rage reveal the filth that lies in the innermost recesses of their hearts. Long before Jude, Isaiah said, "But the wicked are like the tossing sea, which cannot rest, whose waves cast up mire and mud" (Isaiah 57:20). In the hearts of apostates, there is great turmoil because of the mire and filth in their lives. They have no moral restraint, so it is only a matter of time before they reveal the vile and wicked sins that lie hidden deep within their characters.

Throughout the book of Jude, and the Bible as a whole, apostasy and sensual sin go hand in hand. There are many unbelievers who live good, moral lives—but watch out for apostates! They are not simply unbelievers. They know God's truth but turn away from it. In so doing, they open their lives to all sorts of immoral sins, which Jude says are to "their [own] shame." Remember, he wrote that apostates "change the grace of our God into a license for immorality" (4). He wrote, "In a similar way, Sodom and Gomorrah and the surrounding towns gave themselves up to sexual immorality and perversion. They serve as an example" (7). He also wrote, "In the very same way, these dreamers pollute their own bodies" (8). And in verse 13, he compared apostates to raging waves of the sea, "foaming up their [own] shame."

Personally, I have watched many men who knew the truth in their heads, and stood at a sacred desk or a teacher's podium but lacked God's truth in their hearts. They first began to deny the inerrancy of Scripture or the virgin birth. They didn't want to leave "religion," but by and by one went down in divorce, another in adultery, another in homosexuality, or other immorality. It is sad and tragic, but the spirit of apostasy and sensual sin go hand in hand. Sooner or later apostates expose themselves, and the filth of their lives washes up on the shore for everyone to see.

Apostates Lack Purpose

Apostates are easily detected by a lack of peace, a lack of productivity, a lack of proof, a lack of purity, and finally a lack of purpose. In Jude's words, apostates are "wandering stars for whom blackest darkness has been reserved forever" (13). Cosmetic Christians have no real direction in life, no purpose. They are like wandering stars that flash for a while before God darkens their existence.

One of my fondest childhood memories is of lying on my back on a pallet in the backyard of my childhood home on a hot summer night with my family. (That was before the days of air conditioning, color television, and videos. Incidentally, those weren't such bad days. It seems as if families in those days had more time just to lie on pallets in the backyard and spend time with each other.) I will never forget looking up at the stars and learning about the Milky Way, the Big Dipper, and the Little Dipper. We spent hours just gazing into the heavens. And then one dark night, it happened! A shooting star raced across the heavens. Its brilliance was dazzling and then, as quickly as the star had appeared, it disappeared into the darkness of the night sky. I'll never forget the impression it made on my young mind.

God placed all the stars on courses in the heavens. We know this not simply from astronomy but because Scripture reveals, "From the heavens the stars fought, from their courses they fought against Sisera" (Judges 5:20). Stars have orbits, direction, and purpose. That's why stars are important in nocturnal navigation. An experienced sea captain knows the heavens as well as he knows the back of his hand. He simply ignores wandering stars when he sees them because they will make a big flash today and disappear tomorrow. The captain makes nocturnal navigation decisions using stars that have order, ones that are always in their proper places.

Cosmetic Christians, on the other hand, are like shooting stars that lack purpose and direction. They are like burned-out chunks of rock that are hurled into the dark recesses of space. They are stars out of orbit. They do not know where they are going in the Christian life. They have no path, plan, or purpose. Thus they are easily detected by their lack of purpose.

These cosmetic Christians do not want to be in orbit. They do not like structure, nor such things as a statement of faith. They do not want to be fenced in, nor do they want to play within any boundaries. Their battle cry is "soul freedom." Like wandering stars, they will blaze brilliantly for a moment and then plunge off into "the blackest darkness...forever." They will move farther and farther from the source of God's light. Darkness will be the ultimate and bitter end of all who have seen the Light and rejected Him.

Perhaps that is why Jesus said in a parable that they will be cast out into darkness (Matthew 22:13). To me, the blackness of darkness forever is the most haunting aspect about Hell—eternal darkness. How important it is to know we are saved and safe from Hell. Can you imagine how it must be to be conscious and in complete, total darkness forever? When a power failure causes darkness for a few moments, people panic. Just imagine "blackest darkness...forever."

Apostates are not Christians who have lost their salvation. They are cosmetic Christians, who may appear to be "religious," but are lost. They may have light but they lack spiritual life. They try to fool others, but they are like "wandering stars" and lack direction and purpose. How many of us have seen men and women who had much promise and potential blaze brilliantly for a moment and then fall into spiritual darkness? God has His own ways of dealing with cosmetic Christians. False teachers and preachers fall as quickly as they rise. God is still in control!

As we have seen, apostates are easily detected. They cause dissension and are like hidden rocks in our love feasts. They are filled with false promises but, like clouds without rain, have no productivity. They have no fruit and, like trees without fruit, have no proof of their authenticity. Like waves of the sea, they foam up their own shame and reveal their lack of purity. They are without direction, like wandering stars that have no purpose.

What are we to do when we encounter these apostates? It may amaze you to discover that these are the only people in Scripture from whom we are instructed to turn away. Paul wrote to his young preacher friend saying that apostates have "a form of godliness" but deny "its power. Have nothing to do with them" (2 Timothy 3:5).

II. APOSTATES ARE ETERNALLY DOOMED

Like the prophet Amos who cried, "Prepare to meet your God" (Amos 4:12), Jude forewarned of a coming day of judgment when cosmetic Christians will be eternally doomed. He quoted from the prophet Enoch to warn of the doom of apostates (Jude 14-16).

We remember that Enoch "walked with God; then he was no more, because God took him away" (Genesis 5:24). Enoch, who lived during the days preceding the flood, foresaw that the coming of the Lord at the end of our age would be preceded by days of apostasy. He faithfully warned against this apostasy. There is much discussion regarding where Jude obtained his information about Enoch's prophecy, since it is not mentioned elsewhere in Scripture. We need only remember that Jude wrote as he was "moved by the Holy Spirit." Enoch's prophecy is found in the book of Jude because God intended it to be here.[5] "All Scripture is God-breathed and is useful for teaching, rebuking, correcting and training in righteousness" (2 Timothy 3:16).

Enoch lived during the days of Noah, so it is interesting that the Lord Jesus said of His second coming, "As it was in the days of Noah, so it will be at the coming of the Son of Man" (Matthew 24:37). Jesus said that the days that immediately precede His coming again will be like the days of Noah. There were three stages in the days of Noah. First, the people were warned about coming judgment. Then God removed His people from the earth and put them safely into the ark. In the final stage, the judgment of God fell on the earth. And so it will be on that grand and glorious day when Jesus comes again. We are living during days of warning! Faithful preachers are warning the world that the Lord is coming again. Someday God will call out His church at the rapture, and after a time of tribulation the Lord Jesus will come again "to judge everyone."

The Bible says that Enoch "was no more because God took him away." He went to Heaven without dying. He is a picture of the church—of those who will be raptured, who will be taken up into the clouds to meet the Lord in the air. Enoch was taken up, and after this the judgment of God fell. One day after the rapture of the church, the judgment of God will come! Thus, Jude wrote that cosmetic Christians are eternally doomed.

Jude learned three truths from Enoch's prophecy that the Holy

Spirit inspired him to reveal to us: God's judgment is personal; God's judgment is purposeful; and God's judgment is perfect.

God's Judgment is Personal

One of the great truths of the Bible is the second coming of our Lord Jesus. It is also the subject of Enoch's prophecy (Jude 14-15). Jesus is coming again, and His coming will be personal. The early church was looking for Christ in their day. A word constantly escaped their lips, *maranatha,* which means "the Lord cometh." They greeted each other with that word. They shouted that word to each other when they were thrown to lions or burned at the stake.

The second coming of the Lord Jesus Christ is discussed throughout the Bible. Jesus said that He is coming again; "I will come back and take you to be with me that you also may be where I am" (John 14:3). The angels said that He is coming again: "Men of Galilee, . . . why do you stand here looking into the sky? This same Jesus, who has been taken from you into heaven, will come back in the same way you have seen him go into heaven" (Acts 1:11). Paul said, "But our citizenship is in heaven. And we eagerly await a Savior from there, the Lord Jesus Christ" (Philippians 3:20). During the Lord's supper, we remember that, "Whenever you eat this bread and drink this cup, you proclaim the Lord's death until he comes" (1 Corinthians 11:26).

The greatest proof we have that the Bible is true is the way its prophecies have been fulfilled. In Isaiah 7:14, we read that Jesus would be born of a virgin. This prophecy was fulfilled seven hundred years later. Micah wrote five hundred years before Jesus' coming that He would be born in the seemingly insignificant village of Bethlehem. Throughout the Bible, prophecies concerning Christ have unfolded in just the same manner in which they were given. The only major prophecy yet to be fulfilled is the personal return of our Lord Jesus Christ to earth.

In the midst of all this discussion of the second coming, Jude reminds us that one sign of His coming—one of the marks of the last days—will be the rise of cosmetic Christians who slip in secretly. Paul also wrote:

Concerning the coming of our Lord Jesus Christ and our being gathered to him, we ask you, brothers, not to become easily unsettled or alarmed by some prophecy, report or letter supposed to have come from us, saying that the day of the Lord has already come. Don't let anyone deceive you in any way, for that day will not come until the rebellion occurs (2 Thessalonians 2:1-3).

At the rapture, the Lord Jesus will come for us (1 Thessalonians 4:13-18). At the second coming, He will come with us (Jude 14). John, the revelator, glimpsed this coming again of Christ and wrote down a few simple symbols that our finite minds can understand:

I saw heaven standing open and there before me was a white horse, whose rider is called Faithful and True. With justice he judges and makes war. His eyes are like blazing fire, and on his head are many crowns. He has a name written on him that no one knows but he himself. He is dressed in a robe dipped in blood, and his name is the Word of God. The armies of heaven were following him, riding on white horses and dressed in fine linen, white and clean. Out of his mouth comes a sharp sword with which to strike down the nations. "He will rule them with an iron scepter." He treads the wine press of the fury of the wrath of God Almighty. On his robe and on his thigh he has this name written: King of kings and Lord of lords (Revelation 19:11-16).

It is of interest that Enoch, who gave the first prophecy of the second coming and judgment, and John, who gave the last prophecy concerning it (Revelation 22:20), did not speak concerning Christ's first coming that brought salvation. Instead, both Enoch and John dealt with the message of judgment.

Jesus is coming "personally" to judge cosmetic Christians and the chief apostate of them all, the antichrist. The ultimate judgment of God is not going to be World War III, a famine, or a flood. It will be personal. "See, the Lord is coming with thousands upon thousands of his holy ones" (14). Amos said, "Prepare to meet *your* God" (Amos 4:12, italics added). We will all stand before the Lord Jesus Christ, our Savior and Judge.

Jude said, "Behold the Lord comes" (KJV). What a compelling word—"behold." It causes us to stop, to put down what we are doing, and to lift our eyes. John the Baptist used that word when he saw the Lord Jesus coming out of obscurity onto the shore of the Jordan River. He pointed in the Master's direction and said, "Behold the Lamb of God, which taketh away the sin of the world" (John 1:29, KJV). The apostle John used that word when he quoted Jesus standing at the door of the church of Laodicea, saying, "Behold, I stand at the door and knock" (Revelation 3:20, KJV). The word "behold" invites us to draw near. It is little wonder that Jude used it here.

One day our Lord Jesus is coming *personally*. He is not sending Michael, the archangel. He is not sending Moses, the lawgiver. He is not sending Elijah, the prophet. "See, the Lord is coming with thousands upon thousands of his holy ones." What a day that will be when our Jesus we shall see! Fanny Crosby expressed it this way:

> He is coming, the man of sorrows
> Now exalted on high.
> He is coming with loud hosannas
> In the clouds of the sky.
>
> He is coming, our loving Savior,
> Blessed Lamb that was slain,
> In the glory of God the Father
> On the earth He shall reign.
>
> Hallelujah, Hallelujah!
> He is coming again,
> And with joy we shall gather round Him
> At His coming to reign!

God's Judgment is Purposeful

The Bible says that the Lord is coming "to judge everyone" (Jude 15). He is coming for the express purpose of executing judgment. He came the first time to bring salvation. He will come next time to bring judgment. The Bible says, "man is destined to die once, and after that to face judgment" (Hebrews 9:27).

Who is the judge? Jesus said, "The Father judges no one, but has entrusted all judgment to the Son" (John 5:22). The judge is the Lord Jesus who is coming again in person and with purpose. He will be our judge!

If we know Jesus as personal Lord and Savior, we will stand before the judgment seat of Christ after the rapture of the church. Our Lord Jesus plainly tells us that no true believer will ever come into judgment for his or her sins. The true believer's sins were judged in Christ on the cross. He said, "I tell you the truth, whoever hears my word, and believes him who sent me has eternal life, and will not be condemned; he has crossed over from death to life" (John 5:24). We will however appear before the judgment seat (Bema) of Christ to receive our rewards in order that we may lay them at Jesus' feet.

After the rapture and at the second coming of Jesus, He will judge the ungodly. They will stand before the great white judgment throne of God. John glimpsed it and revealed what he saw:

> Then I saw a great white throne and him who was seated on it. Earth and sky fled from his presence, and there was no place for them. And I saw the dead, great and small, standing before the throne, and books were opened. Another book was opened, which is the book of life. The dead were judged according to what they had done as recorded in the books. The sea gave up the dead that were in it, and death and Hades gave up the dead that were in them, and each person was judged according to what he had done. Then death and Hades were thrown into the lake of fire. The lake of fire is the second death. If anyone's name was not found written in the book of life, he was thrown into the lake of fire (Revelation 20:11-15).

This is the judgment about which Jude wrote in verses 14-15. In the context of this judgment, we read the word "ungodly" four times. Ungodly people, not the saved, will stand before the great white throne of God. Jesus is coming personally for the express purpose of executing judgment on the "ungodly." The verb used is a Greek infinitive of purpose, which means Jesus is coming for the express purpose of judgment. No one will escape. Just as judgment by the flood destroyed everyone outside the ark, the final judgment will encompass all the ungodly. Just as the fire and brimstone that fell during the judgment of Sodom destroyed everyone in the city except Lot, his wife, and daughters, so will the final judgment encompass all the ungodly. They won't be able to hide. Their alibis won't work. They won't escape.

God's Judgment is Perfect

Jude concluded his words on cosmetic Christians by revealing that Christ's judgment will be perfect. The Lord Jesus is coming purposefully "to convict all the ungodly of all the ungodly acts they have done in the ungodly way" (Jude 15). Our legal courts, at best, are imperfect. Many innocent people have been convicted, and many guilty people have gone free. But the judgment of God will be perfect! He knows who is wearing a mask and who isn't. He knows who is cosmetic and who is committed. He knows the synthetic saints from the sincere saints.

In God's perfect judgment, the Lord Jesus Himself will be the judge. There will be no jury or prosecution. There will be no defense. Every mouth will be silenced. The Bible says, "Now we know that whatever the law says, it says to those who are under the law, so that every mouth may be silenced and the whole world held accountable to God" (Romans 3:19). There will be a sentence but no appeal. There is no higher court at the great white throne of God. Why? The Lord's judgment and sentence are perfect. In fact, the verdict and sentence are found in Matthew 25:41: "Then he will say to those on his left, 'depart from me, you who are cursed, into the eternal fire prepared for the devil and his angels.'" God is just. The Bible says, "Will not the Judge of all the earth do right?" (Genesis 18:25)

There will be degrees of punishment in Hell. Our Lord Jesus alluded to this when He said in the cursing of the three cities of Galilee:

Woe to you, Korazin! Woe to you, Bethsaida! If the miracles that were performed in you had been performed in Tyre and

Sidon, they would have repented long ago in sackcloth and ashes. But I tell you, it will be more bearable for Tyre and Sidon on the day of judgment than for you. And you, Capernaum, will you be lifted up to the skies? No, you will go down to the depths. If the miracles that were performed in you had been performed in Sodom, it would have remained to this day. But I tell you that it will be more bearable for Sodom on the day of judgment than for you (Matthew 11:21-24).

Those in Hell who lived in Sodom will find it different from those who heard Christ in the Galilean cities mentioned here. Our Lord also said:

That servant who knows his master's will and does not get ready or does not do what his master wants will be beaten with many blows. But the one who does not know and does things deserving punishment will be beaten with few blows. From everyone who has been given much, much will be demanded; and from the one who has been entrusted with much, much more will be asked (Luke 12:47-48).

Jesus seems to indicate by these comments that there will be a difference in the intensity of Hell's punishment.

What will Jesus judge? He will judge sins of action—"ungodly acts they have done" (Jude 15). People who do not know Christ will give an account at the great white throne of God for everything they've ever done.

Those who are eternally lost will also give an account for sins of the tongue, "harsh words ungodly sinners have spoken against him" (Jude 15). Jesus said, "But I tell you that men will have to give account on that day of judgment for every careless word they have spoken" (Matthew 12:36). Jude said that cosmetic Christians grumble about the authority of the Word of God. They are discontented with the life God has given them. They are "faultfinders," blaming everything and everyone for their lot in life (Jude 16).

Faultfinding is a common characteristic of those who have turned their backs on God's truth. One day they will stand before God to answer for sins of the tongue. Jude wrote that apostates "boast about themselves and flatter others for their own advantage" (16.)

Their words are empty. Anyone who has heard the verbosity of cosmetic Christians needs no further explanation. Many people have been fooled by men and women who had great words, but cosmetic Christians have not fooled God! He will judge their actions and their words.

The Lord will also judge sins of thought. In Jude's words, apostates "follow their own evil desires" (16). The spiritual battle takes place in the mind. Remember the Bible says, "Anyone, then, who knows the good he ought to do and doesn't do it, sins" (James 4:17). These are sins of omission. God knows our motives and thoughts. These sins too will be judged by the Lord Jesus Himself.

The Bible plainly teaches there are only two destinies for mankind: Heaven and Hell. Those who go to Hell will stand before the perfect judgment seat of God, the degree of their punishment will be decided, and they will be eternally doomed. That is one reason why the book of Jude is so vital today. Apostates—cosmetic Christians—will suffer more than others because they know the truth and have turned from it. This is a real warning to anyone reading these words who knows the will and the way of God but as yet has not acted upon them. Hell's hottest section is reserved for those who know, yet still reject God's truth. Like bank robbers and others who disguise themselves to cover their true identities, apostates are cosmetic. They are easily detected and eternally doomed. Although they may try to put on enough spiritual makeup to appear to be Christians, God sees through them and says, "I never knew you; depart from me."

So what should our response be during these days? We are to receive forgiveness under the blood of Christ through repentance and faith. What a difference there will be between the judgment seat of Christ for the Christian and the great white throne for the lost. How thankful we who are saved should be that "we have an advocate with the Father, Jesus Christ the righteous" (1 John 2:1). How thankful we should be as we read Edward Mote's famous hymn:

> My hope is built on nothing less
> Than Jesus' blood and righteousness;
> I dare not trust the sweetest frame,
> But wholly lean on Jesus' name.

> When He shall come with trumpet sound,
> O may I then in Him be found;
> Dressed in His righteousness alone,
> Faultless to stand before the throne.

The last prophecy and promise of the Bible comes from the lips of our Lord: "Yes, I am coming soon" (Revelation 22:20). John voiced the last prayer in the Bible, which is also found in this same verse: "Come, Lord Jesus." In light of events that we see coming to pass, we join John the revelator in praying, "Even so, come, Lord Jesus."

During these last days, may the church awaken and not be fooled by the cosmetic appearances of apostates. They are like a hidden rock, a cloud without rain, a tree without fruit, a raging wave of the sea, and a wandering star. The church should be on the lookout for those who would destroy the fellowship of love, who would promise so much and produce so little, who never produce fruit, whose lives are filled with filth, and who flash and fade away without direction. They will face the judgment of God, and we will be responsible if the foundations be destroyed.

CHAPTER SEVEN
Apostasy Viewed Sympathetically

But, dear friends, remember what the apostles of our Lord Jesus Christ foretold. They said to you, "In the last times there will be scoffers who will follow their own ungodly desires." These are the men who divide you, who follow mere natural instincts and do not have the Spirit. But you, dear friends, build yourselves up in your most holy faith and pray in the Holy Spirit. Keep yourselves in God's love as you wait for the mercy of our Lord Jesus Christ to bring you to eternal life. Be merciful to those who doubt; snatch others from the fire and save them; to others show mercy, mixed with fear—hating even the clothing stained by corrupted flesh (Jude 17-23).

I. BE EDUCATED
II. BE INSULATED
III. BE DEDICATED

It has been somewhat depressing to read of the apostasy during the last days revealed throughout Jude's Epistle. Perhaps you are asking yourself, *what can I do about it?* In dealing with the apostasy we have read about thus far, it may seem as though there is little hope. But note the way Jude begins verse 17: "But." This word denotes a reversal.

In verses 17-23 of his letter, Jude showed us how to deal with apostasy in a sympathetic sense by calling us to three very important matters. First, he said we should be educated as to who the apostate is, what he does, and why he does it. Second, he called on us to be insulated by keeping ourselves in the love of God. Finally, during these days of apostasy, he warned us to be dedicated as a warm living sacrifice that bears a compassionate, courageous, and cautious witness to those who don't know Christ personally. In verse 22, Jude admonished us, in the midst of our defense of the faith, to remember to "be merciful." There is a sense in which we need to deal with apostasy in a sympathetic sense.

I. BE EDUCATED

Jude wrote, "But dear friends, remember what the apostles of our Lord Jesus Christ foretold" (17). He called us to look back to the words of the apostles because the way to move forward in our Christian growth is not by means of modern innovations or future revelations but by recalling what has been previously revealed to the apostles.[1] The truth is, if the words are new, they are not true. Remember, this faith has been "once for all entrusted to the saints" (Jude 3). That is why we need to familiarize ourselves with "what the apostles of our Lord Jesus Christ foretold." One of the important ministries of the Holy Spirit is to "bring all things to your remembrance" (John 14:26). However, information cannot be brought to our remembrance if it has never been deposited in our minds. There is no substitute for being knowledgeable about the Word of God.

What did the apostles say? In Paul's farewell speech to the church at Ephesus, he said, "I know that after I leave, savage wolves will come in among you, and will not spare the flock" (Acts 20:29). To Timothy, his son in the ministry, Paul wrote, "The Spirit clearly says that in later times some will abandon the faith and follow deceiving spirits and things taught by demons" (1 Timothy 4:1). Simon Peter, the big fisherman, wrote, "First of all, you must understand that in the last days scoffers [mockers] will come, scoffing and following their own evil desires" (2 Peter 3:3). Remembering these words confirms Jude's message.

Another aspect of our education concerns three key questions about apostates that we must answer in dealing with apostasy in a sympathetic sense. Every true believer needs to know who apostates are, what they do, and why they do it.

Who are Apostates?

Jude tells us they are "scoffers...who will follow their own ungodly desires" (18). The apostles spoke similar words when they told us that mockers would be prevalent during the last days.

In the midst of all the apostasy today, some people are saying, "Well, perhaps the Bible is not the inerrant, trustworthy, and infallible revelation of God after all." Many discredit Scripture and claim it is not true. Many say that it contains the word of God but is not the Word of God. The truth is, every professor in every school who denies the inerrancy of the Word of God is proving it to be true. The Bible says that we should expect these mockers during the last days. In the words of Jude, there will be "scoffers who will follow their own ungodly desires."

The Greek word rendered "mocker" in the King James Version is interesting. It means to "act in a childish fashion, to be childish, to play." There is a world of difference in being childish and childlike. The Lord Jesus said, "Unless you...become like little children, you will never enter the kingdom of heaven" (Matthew 18:3). The Lord honors childlikeness but abhors childishness. Apostates are childish in behavior because they mock the gospel and Christians. This behavior certainly is not novel or new.

We should not be surprised if we are mocked, because our Lord was mocked. The most heartbreaking thing to me about Jesus' experience on the cross is not the fact that they beat Him with a whip until His back was a bloody pulp, nor the fact that they spit into His face, nor that they plucked His beard with their hands, nor that they slapped and beat Him on the head with a reed, nor even that they nailed Him to the cruel, Roman cross. The thing that grieves me the most is that they stripped Him naked, put a scarlet robe on Him, plaited a crown of thorns and pressed it upon His brow, and then bowed in front of Him and mocked Him. They laughed and laughed and laughed.

Mockers treat the Word (living or written) in open defiance! Those who mock Scripture today are no different from those who mocked the living Word Himself! These mockers "follow their own ungodly desires" (Jude 18). In other words, they are slaves to sin and self, to their ungodliness and lusts. This explains why they deny God's truth. They do not want God to tell them how to live.

What do apostates do?

Jude goes on to tell us that we should be educated as to *what* apostates do: "These are the men, who divide you, who follow mere natural instincts" (19). If by now we have not been able to distinguish apostate believers from authentic believers, Jude gives us this additional description.

Jude first pointed out that apostates cause divisions. I have noticed division taking place in the current battle for the Bible. When someone believes the Bible is "truth, without any mixture of error," and rises up against the apostasy of the day, he or she is usually labeled a troublemaker and is accused of being divisive. But the Bible believers are not causing division. Jude wrote that the apostates cause division. They can lay the blame on others with accusations of narrow-mindedness and intolerance until they are blue in the face, but the Bible is crystal clear in its revelation that apostates are the guilty ones.

Division commonly occurs during days of apostasy. There are many illustrations of this, not the least of which is the division in the Presbyterian and Lutheran churches in recent years. True believers, who in good conscience can no longer support apostate teachings, have had to establish new churches and, in some cases, even new denominations to preserve Biblical truth for posterity.

Jude goes on to say that apostates "follow [their] mere natural instincts". The King James Version uses the word "sensual" in Jude 19 to describe Apostates. Again we are reminded that apostasy and sensual sins are linked together. Apostates "change the grace of our God into a license for immorality." They "gave themselves up to sexual immorality and perversion." They "defile the flesh." They are like "raging waves of the sea, foaming up their own shame." To sum it up, they are "sensual."

The word "sensual" is derived from the Greek word *psychikos*. It means "limited to the senses, limited to the soul."[2] Man is comprised of spirit, soul, and body, and it is the spirit part of him that can commune with God. For the unsaved person—the one who is dead spiritually without Christ—the best he or she can do is to operate on a soulish level—that is, they are controlled by their sensuous appetites, passions and affections. The apostate is worldly minded and sensual. There is nothing about him or her that is spiritual. He operates and makes decisions based solely on his selfish ambitions and desires. He walks according to his own ungodly lusts.

One of the tragedies of today's superficial Christianity is that many people cannot discern between spiritual ministries and soulish ministries that appeal to the seat of our emotions only.

Spiritual ministries edify; soulish ministries entertain. Spiritual ministries seek the applause and amen of God; soulish ministries seek the applause of men and women. Synthetic saints can function only in the soulish realm. They do not have the Spirit (19).

True believers seeking to deal with the spirit of apostasy in a sympathetic sense initially need to be educated concerning the identities and actions of apostates —who they are and what they do.

Why Apostates Act As They Do

Next, true believers need to be educated concerning why apostates do what they do. Why are they immoral in body? Why are they insubordinate in soul? Why are they irreverent in spirit? Why are they sensual? Why do they cause division? Why are they mockers? Why do they walk according to their ungodly lusts? The answer is plainly before us. They "do not have the Spirit" (19). This fact alone should break our hearts. That is why I describe this section of verses in terms of dealing with apostasy sympathetically.

Since the Holy Spirit is not resident in apostates' lives, nothing about them is spiritual. Therefore no matter how much apostates profess with their lips to being Christians, they are not authentic, genuine believers. Jude made it perfectly clear that apostates are not Christians when he wrote that they "do not have the Spirit." Paul expressed it this way: "If any one does not have the Spirit of Christ, he does not belong to Christ" (Romans 8:9).

How thankful we as true believers should be that "God sent the Spirit of his Son into our hearts" (Galatians 4:6). No wonder Paul wrote, "Christ in you, the hope of glory" (Colossians 1:27). This is the difference between synthetic saints and sincere saints. This is the root reason why apostates are what they are and do what they do!

It is important for us to be educated concerning apostasy. When we are, this knowledge should move us to be sympathetic and not hostile toward apostates.

II. BE INSULATED

In dealing with apostasy we must not only be educated. We must also be insulated. What is our insulation during days of apostasy?

It is the love of God! Jude wrote, "keep yourselves in God's love" (21). This is what our Lord was referring to during the evening before the crucifixion when He admonished us saying, "remain in my love" (John 15:9). We are to keep ourselves in the love of God, which is our insulation during days of apostasy. By the way, notice that Jude did not write, "Keep on loving God." The issue here is not our love for God, but His love for us.

How can we know God's love? Paul revealed it to us when he wrote that he wanted us to know the love of Christ that passes knowledge and described four ways to do so. He referred to the width and length and depth and height of God's love (Ephesians 3:18).

The breadth of God's love is evidenced in the fact that "God so loved the world that he gave his one and only Son, that whoever believes in him shall not perish but have eternal life" (John 3:16). God loves everyone.

The length of His love is evidenced in the fact that none of us can sin ourselves out of the love of God; He just keeps on loving us.

The depth of His love is seen in the fact that He came down, past solar systems and constellations, to become as helpless as a tiny seed planted in the virgin's womb. And then He demonstrated His own love toward us in that "while we were still sinners, Christ died for us" (Romans 5:8).

The height of His love is seen in the fact that He has raised us and "seated us...in the heavenly realms in Christ Jesus" (Ephesians 2:6). As the songwriter, Charles H. Gabriel wrote, "From sinking sand He lifted me,/ With tender hand He lifted me." It is in this love that Jude said we are to "keep" ourselves.

The key to keeping ourselves in the love of God is found when we carefully observe these words chosen by Jude: "keep yourselves in God's love." The burden is on us! Although it is true that God keeps us from "stumbling" on the divine side of the equation, there is also the human side to consider. What does it mean to keep ourselves in His love? How can we do it? The best illustration is found in Luke 15 in the well-known and often-repeated story of the prodigal son.

A lad took his inheritance and left the comfort and protection of his father's love to journey into a "far country." Once there, he wasted all he had in wild living and ended up in a pigpen, longing to eat the husks of corn the pigs were eating. All the while, back at home his father lovingly and patiently awaited the day when his son would come home. We all know the happy ending—the reconciliation and rejoicing. Longfellow calls this the greatest short story ever written.

The relationship of this parable to God's love is simple. When the prodigal left home, it did not mean that his father stopped loving him. It did however mean that the son had stepped outside of the environment of that love. While the young man was away, his father's love for him never changed. His father still loved him. What had changed was that the young man had removed himself from the place of blessing and the benefit of his father's love.[3]

The same truth applies to us. Many of us have removed ourselves from the place of blessing and love and no longer abide in the love of God. We can know nothing of God's love when we travel to a "far country." All we have there are memories of bygone days. When the prodigal returned home, he again experienced his father's love. It is the same with us. To keep ourselves "in God's love" means to stay in His will and be what He wants us to be.

Every believer needs to stay in God's love during the days of apostasy. We need to be insulated. Three important words in these verses give us the secret of being insulated by the love of God: build, pray, and wait. These verbs describe how we are to keep ourselves in the love of God.[4]

The Inward Look of Edification

"Build yourselves up in your most holy faith" (20). Our "most holy faith" is the same thing as "the faith" mentioned in verse 3. "The faith" is that which is believed—the complete body of Biblical doctrine that comprises the perfect whole of God's written truth. It is the full and final revelation of God as we have it in the Scriptures. "The faith" is the Bible! We are to stay insulated by keeping ourselves in the love of Christ, and the first step in doing this is to build ourselves up in our most holy faith—the Word of God.

I am convinced that the key to understanding this principle in Jude's text is often overlooked. Notice that he wrote, *"Your* most holy faith" (italics added). When we receive the Lord Jesus, what is His becomes ours. His Word becomes ours. All the promises of God are ours. The most holy faith becomes ours. Remember, we are custodians of this most holy faith, which was "once for all entrusted to the saints" (3).

Jude next admonished us to build ourselves up in this most holy faith. We should be studying the Word of God for ourselves. We will never build ourselves up in this most holy faith if the only time we study the Word is at church when the preacher is preaching, in the classroom when the teacher is teaching, in front of the television or radio when the speaker is speaking, or even when we read what others have written. The only way we can build ourselves up in this most holy faith is to explore the Word of God for ourselves.

I know some people who study the Bible, and I know other people who know some people who study the Bible. If all we get out of the Bible is what God has given someone else who has dug into the Word, we'll never be built up in the Word of God. Too many Christians today read books about the Bible rather than reading the Word itself. If we are not built up in the Word of God, we'll never be insulated by keeping ourselves in His love.

After pastoring the church in Ephesus for three years, Paul was called of God to spread the Gospel throughout the Mediterranean world. One of the most touching scenes in Scripture is found in Acts 20, when the believers came down to the shore to see him leave on the ship. They wept together. His parting words to these people whom he had led to Christ and taught to grow were these:

> Keep watch over yourselves and all the flock of which the Holy Spirit has made you overseers. Be shepherds of the church of God, which he bought with his own blood. I know that after I leave, savage wolves will come in among you and will not spare the flock. Even from your own number men will arise and distort the truth in order to draw away disciples after them. So be on your guard! Remember that for three years I never stopped warning each of you night and day with tears. Now I commit you to God and to the word of his grace, which can build you up and give you an inheritance among all those who are sanctified (Acts 20:28-32).

Paul pointed these believers to the Word of God that was able to "build" them up.[5] Peter also wrote: "Like newborn babies, crave pure spiritual milk, so that by it you may grow up in your salvation" (1 Peter 2:2).

The first step in being insulated in God's love is to build ourselves up in the Word of God. This is the inward look of edification. Realizing this, Paul also wrote to his young preacher friend, Timothy, "All Scripture is God-breathed and is useful for teaching, rebuking, correcting and training in righteousness, so that the man of God may be thoroughly equipped for every good work" (2 Timothy 3:16-17).

During these days, when so many people are questioning the authority of Scripture and the assaults of higher criticism are being leveled against the Book of God, it is important to remember that it is a "most holy" book. To Jude, the Bible did not simply contain the Word of God. It was the Word of God—sacred, holy, set apart by God, supernatural in origin, and divine in nature. Authentic Christians do not worship the Bible, but they honor and respect it as being "most holy."

The inward look of edification is obtained only through the Word of God. Jesus said, "If you remain in me and my words remain in you, ask whatever you wish, and it will be given you" (John 15:7). It is His will—in us—that builds us up and keeps us in the love of God. We cannot be insulated without the Bible.

The Upward Look of Supplication

No matter how grounded we may be in the Word of God, we will be defeated if we seek to overcome apostasy in our own strength. We need the upward look of supplication—that is, we need to "pray in the Holy Spirit" (Jude 20). Not many of us today know much about praying in the Holy Spirit. (Quite honestly, I am far more knowledgeable experientially about building up myself in the Word of God than I am about praying in the Holy Spirit.)

I am convinced that one of modern-day Christianity's biggest blessings is, in many ways, one of its most subtle dangers. We are overwhelmed by printed materials concerning our Christian faith. Christian bookstores are some of the fastest-growing businesses in America. We can walk into any Christian bookstore and find dozens of books and tapes about prayer. We are preoccupied with the instructions yet seldom put them into practice.

In the book of Acts we read about the greatest prayer warriors of all time. Those early believers called down God's power from Heaven and opened prison doors solely with prayer. They never read a book titled *How to Pray,* but they knew that the shortest way to a person's heart is through the throne of grace. They never attended a prayer seminar. They did not even listen to a tape series on prayer. They simply prayed in the Holy Spirit. And when they did so, the power of God came down! Today we know all about prayer in theory, but not enough of us know about it in experience.

Many of us need to ask our Lord to do what the disciples asked Him to do so long ago on a Galilean hillside: "Lord, teach us to pray" (Luke 11:1). Amazingly this is the only thing the disciples asked Jesus to teach them to do. They never said, "Lord, teach us to preach," or "Lord, teach us to evangelize." They never said, "Lord, teach us to administrate," or "Lord, teach us to perform social ministries." Having lived with Him for three and a half years, they knew that the power of His life was generated during the time He spent alone with His Father in prayer. They knew that if they could learn to pray as Jesus prayed, then preaching with power and meeting the needs of the ministry would result. Oh, that we would join in asking God to teach us to pray. The disciples did not ask, "Lord, teach us how to pray." Most of us know how to pray; we just do not pray! Our hope of being insulated in God's love during days of apostasy lies in praying in the Holy Spirit.

What does it mean to "pray in the Holy Spirit"? Some would say this phrase refers to "ecstatic utterance." But there is no basis for this interpretation within the Epistle of Jude. Rather this phrase has to do with what Jack Taylor calls the "cycle of prayer" in his classic book, *Prayer: Life's Limitless Reach.* Taylor points out that true prayer does not begin with us but at the throne of God. The Bible says that "we do not know what we ought to pray for" (Romans 8:26). Therefore God takes the initiative and impresses on our hearts, through His Spirit and often through His Word, the requests for which we should pray. Since we "do not know what we ought to pray for," the apostle Paul continued his explanation by saying,

But the Spirit himself intercedes for us with groans that words cannot express. And he who searches our hearts knows the mind of the Spirit, because the Spirit intercedes for the saints in accordance with God's will (Romans 8:26-27).

Therefore Jude's admonition to us to "pray in the Holy Spirit" reveals several truths. We are dependent on the guidance of the Holy Spirit in our lives in order to know for what we ought to pray. Because we do not know the future we are dependent on God for direction, just as a child is dependent on a parent for guidance. Also we need the Spirit's help in prayer to keep our motives pure. Paul wrote, "Your attitude should be the same as that of Christ Jesus" (Philippians 2:5). The only way we can pray with the attitude of Christ is to "pray in the Holy Spirit." Often we are so taken up with articulating our prayers that we cease to pray and simply begin to "say prayers." There is a level of prayer that goes beyond mere words. I refer to it as the prayer of communion, or the prayer that the Holy Spirit prays through us as we commune with the Father.

We need the Spirit's help in prayer so that we might pray according to the will of God. John revealed, "This is the confidence we have in approaching God: that if we ask anything according to his will, he hears us. And if we know that he hears us—whatever we ask—we know that we have what we asked of him" (1 John 5:14-15).[6] Our Lord Himself prayed in Gethsemane's garden, saying "not my will, but yours, be done" (Luke 22:42).

Some people pray in the flesh, according to their worldly desires. No wonder their prayers are not answered. James expressed it this way: "When you ask, you do not receive, because you ask with wrong motives, that you may spend what you get on your pleasures" (James 4:3). Others pray in the soulish realm, according to their passions and feelings. They become worked up emotionally but have nothing left after "the experience" has passed away. The prayer that keeps us "in God's love" however, is prayer in the Spirit. That is the way we become spiritually insulated. The Word of God and prayer keep us in the love of God, which is our insulation during days of apostasy.

It is wonderfully assuring to know that, at the right hand of the Father, the Lord Jesus is always making intercession for us. At the same time, within us, the Holy Spirit is making intercession for the saints according to the will of God. We are totally dependent on

Him. We are called, loved, and kept by Him. Even now, Jesus is praying for us, ever living to make intercession for us.

It is not enough for us simply to be educated. During these days of apostasy we will go down in defeat if we are not insulated in the love of God through the Word of God and through prayer. Both are vitally important and are meant to go together. The Bible without prayer has no dynamic; prayer without the Bible has no direction. Just as it is not enough for us to be educated without being insulated, it is also not enough for us to read the Word of God without praying.

The Forward Look of Anticipation

Many believers never get past the cross in their Christian experience. It is important to look back in appreciation, but it is also important to look forward in anticipation. In the words of Jude, "Wait for the mercy of our Lord Jesus Christ to bring you to eternal life" (21). In order to be insulated in the love of God during these days of apostasy, it is not enough to look back. As believers we have something for which to look forward. Jude alluded to the second coming of Christ here because apostasy is one of the major signs of the last days that signal the Lord's return. It is not enough to build ourselves up in the Word of God and pray in the Holy Spirit. We must also eagerly anticipate the return of our Savior, the Lord Jesus Christ. Paul referred to this great event when he wrote, "While we wait for the blessed hope—the glorious appearing of our great God and Savior, Jesus Christ" (Titus 2:13).

Today few who profess Christ seem to be looking for Jesus. In fact, some believers even give the impression that mentioning the second coming is a bit old-fashioned. Earlier in this book we considered how seldom the blood of Christ is being preached in modern-day pulpits. Sadly I fear the same is true with respect to the doctrine of His "glorious appearing." Not many of us live with the anticipation that Jesus might return today. Jude reveals that this is one reason why some people are not keeping themselves in the love of God. They have lost their forward look of anticipation.

As believers we should be looking for our Savior, the Lord Jesus Christ. Doing so makes a difference in the way we live. When we

sincerely look for Christ to return at any time, we become motivated to live godly lives. Anticipating Jesus' return leads us to a
lifestyle of godliness and expectation. The way to keep insulated is
to keep our eyes on Jesus who said, "If I go..., I will come back and
take you to be with me" (John 14:3). This forward look helps to keep
us in the love of God.

All of these words—build, pray, wait—should continually characterize our behavior. If we expect to be insulated in the love of
God, we should continually study the Bible. We should continually
pray in the Holy Spirit. We should continually look for the return of
our Savior, the Lord Jesus Christ. The inward look of edification,
the upward look of supplication, and the forward look of anticipation will keep us in the love of God, which is our insulation during
days of apostasy. Many persons who were educated about apostasy have fallen because they were not insulated in the love of God.

III. BE DEDICATED

It is not enough to be educated and insulated if we are not
dedicated. This dedication exhibits itself as a warm, living sacrifice
taken up with love for the lost. Paul put it this way:

> Therefore, I urge you, brothers, in view of God's mercy, to
> offer your bodies as living sacrifices, holy and pleasing to
> God—this is your spiritual act of worship. Do not conform any
> longer to the pattern of this world, but be transformed by the
> renewing of your mind. Then you will be able to test and
> approve what God's will is—his good, pleasing and perfect
> will (Romans 12:1-2).

Likewise, Jude wrote, "Be merciful to those who doubt; snatch
others from the fire and save them; to others show mercy, mixed
with fear—hating even the clothing stained by corrupted flesh"
(Jude 22-23).

The church today is often too silent with its witness. I am
convinced that we should respond to those who are influenced by
the spirit of apostasy in a sympathetic way. One of the most
hypocritical things in the world is orthodoxy without compassion.

Many people who speak the truth today do not do so in love. Our admonition from Paul is to speak the truth in love (Ephesians 4:15). Jude admonished us to be compassionate soul winners, and the best way for us to do this is to live a devoted life that is a warm, living sacrifice.

The problem with many Christians today is that they have lost their compassion for unsaved people. The reason is that so few Christians live separated lives, and many have lost their tears. Once a young captain in the Salvation Army wrote to General Booth, the godly and soul-winning founder, saying, "I'm not seeing any converts. People do not seem to be responding to my message." General Booth replied by telegram with only two words: "Try tears." There is a dire need for Christians living during these days of apostasy to cry tears as they deal with the lost sympathetically.

According to Jude, three groups of people need our witness: sincere doubters, those who live on the very edge of Hell, and those who are deeply contaminated by sin. In other words, we need to deal with some people compassionately, some people courageously, and still others cautiously.

Compassionate Witness

In dealing with those influenced by a spirit of apostasy, we should deal with some people compassionately. Jude wrote, "Be merciful to those who doubt." We should approach those who sincerely doubt in a compassionate way. We remember well the story of Simon Peter, who walked on the water at Christ's invitation (Matthew 14). He started out and did well until fear gripped his heart. As doubt began to set in, he began to sink and cried out, "Lord save me!" Jesus reached out His hand and asked, "Oh you of little faith, why did you doubt?" Many people today, like Peter, are slowly sinking. Oh, that more of God's people would reach out to them today and have compassion.

Right belief is useless if it lacks compassion. Someone has said, "People do not care how much we know until they know how much we care." The word *mercy* in the NIV is translated *compassion* in the KJV. The word *compassion* comes from two Latin words: *com,* which means "with," and *passion,* which means "to suffer." Therefore, *compassion* literally means to "put oneself in the place of another; to suffer with that person." It is becoming one of the lost words of our Christian vocabulary.

Many Christians today see others in the same manner as the man whom Jesus touched in Mark 8. This blind man could see with the first touch, but he said, "I see people; they look like trees walking around." He could not see clearly. So blurred was this man's vision that he could not tell a man from a tree. He could not tell if a man was wearing a coat. He could not tell if a man was bald or had a full head of hair. He couldn't see a person's back bent with a burden. He couldn't see quivering lips. He couldn't see ragged and frayed clothes. He couldn't see a stomach that was bloated from malnutrition. He couldn't see bare feet. He couldn't see a dirty face. He couldn't see tearful eyes. Hence, if he couldn't see a tearful eye, he couldn't wipe the eyes of a tearful person. If he couldn't see a dirty face, he could not clean the face of a dirty person. If he couldn't see feet that were bare, he couldn't put shoes on them. If he couldn't see a back that was bent with a burden, he couldn't lighten the person's load.

Need I say more? Too many of us are only interested in our jobs, our churches, our families, our pain, our theology, and our orthodoxy. We focus on words such as *me, mine,* and *ours!* We are no different from the blind man mentioned in the Bible. We see people without really seeing them. But when Jesus touched the blind man a second time, he "saw everything clearly." During these days of apostasy, we all need the touch of Jesus that helps us to reach out with compassion. When we are educated, insulated, and dedicated to God, we can deal with others compassionately.

Sincere doubters are not necessarily antagonistic toward the Gospel, they are just not sure about it. They have doubts, but they are sincere. Sincere doubters simply do not know any better. Incidentally, this type of person begins listening to Mormons, Jehovah Witnesses, or other cults. This is all the more reason why genuine Christians should show great compassion when dealing with these people and pressing the claims of Christ to their hearts.

We need to have our hearts broken in compassion over the plight of the lost. There are those about us who honestly do not know what to believe. These precious ones need to be dealt with compassionately in patience and perseverance. It is impossible to be dedicated to God, as a warm, living sacrifice, and have compassion if we are not insulated though the Word, prayer, and the anticipated hope of His glorious appearing.

Courageous witness

Other people are to be dealt with courageously. Jude wrote, "snatch others from the fire and save them" (23). This group is farther away from God than those who are sincere doubters. They need to be pulled out of the fire because they are obviously closer to the flames of Hell. It takes a much stronger and bolder stand to witness to this type of individual. Believers should approach them courageously. No case should be regarded as hopeless because no one is beyond the reach of God. However, to reclaim those so near the fire, a real sense of urgency is needed. Just as a man plucks a burning stick out of the fire, this individual needs to be dealt with boldly and courageously.

The fire about which Jude wrote in these verses is eternal fire. He alluded to it earlier in verse 7 when he wrote that the inhabitants of Sodom and Gomorrah were given to us "as an example of those who suffer the punishment of eternal fire." It is amazing how silent most pulpits are regarding the Biblical doctrine of Hell. Let me quote what one preacher said about Hell:

> Do not be afraid of those who kill the body but cannot kill the soul. Rather, be afraid of the One who can destroy both soul and body in hell (Matthew 10:28).
>
> The Son of Man will send out his angels, and they will weed out of his kingdom everything that causes sin and all who do evil. They will throw them into the fiery furnace, where there will be weeping and gnashing of teeth (Matthew 13:41-42).
>
> Then he will say to those on his left, 'Depart from me, you who are cursed, into the eternal fire prepared for the devil and his angels' (Matthew 25:41).
>
> Then they will go away to eternal punishment, but the righteous to eternal life (Matthew 25:46).

Who was this preacher? The Lord Jesus Himself! In fact, He spent far more time warning about the dangers of Hell than He did speaking about the glories of Heaven. The Lord Jesus chose to use the word "fire" to describe the punishment of those who do not know Christ personally.

Jude wrote that if we really are sympathetic, we will have courage and be bold in snatching those who live on the edge of Hell from the fire. If we really believe what the Bible teaches about Hell, we will want to bring eternally lost people to Jesus Christ. The problem today however is that some Christians are not sure what they believe about Hell. General Booth said that he wished he could send all of his candidates for Salvation Army officership to Hell for twenty-four hours as part of their training. He was convinced that only in this way would they develop the compassion needed to seek the lost and the courage needed to snatch them from the fire. Surely this is what Fanny Crosby had in mind when she penned these penetrating words:

> Rescue the perishing, care for the dying,
> Snatch them in pity from sin and the grave;
> Weep o'er the erring one, lift up the fallen,
> Tell them of Jesus, the mighty to save.
>
> Down in the human heart, crushed by the tempter,
> Feelings lie buried that grace can restore;
> Touched by a loving heart, wakened by kindness,
> Cords that are broken will vibrate once more.
>
> Rescue the perishing, duty demands it—
> Strength for your labor the Lord will provide;
> Back to the narrow way patiently win them,
> Tell the poor wan-d'rer a Savior has died.
>
> Rescue the perishing, Care for the dying;
> Jesus is merciful, Jesus will save.

Cautious witness

There are others with whom we should deal cautiously. Jude wrote, "to others show mercy, mixed with fear—hating even the clothing stained by corrupted flesh" (23). Those who have departed the faith are to be approached with "fear." We are warned to be cautious, lest we ourselves be trapped (See 1 Corinthians 10:12). Some sins and sinners do not merely threaten the spiritual life of the soul winner but may actually snare him or her. More than one well-meaning man or woman who had a heart for God and thought he could stand firm has fallen into the trap of Satan when trying to witness to those whose garments were "stained by corrupted flesh."

Jude warned us that we must love people but hate ungodly lifestyles. In fact, he warned that we should hate even the garments that are polluted by sin. Certainly we should deal with people compassionately and courageously, but we must also remember to be cautious. We should never let our compassion and courage overshadow our caution!

Jude revealed to us that even men and women who have sunk into sin and into a spirit of apostasy are not to be abandoned.[7] The outright apostate is the only one of whom the Bible says to turn away. Those about whom Jude wrote in the concluding verses of his text should be dealt with sympathetically, yet cautiously.

Some people think the way to win the social elite to Christ is to compromise their lifestyles. However we should never compromise in order to win someone to Christ. We are called to be separate (2 Corinthians 6:14-18). From time to time, we hear about someone who seeks to justify sin in order to "win over the sinner." But we never find that principle in the Bible. More than one Christian who sought to justify his or her sin in order to win someone else, has fallen.

Some Christians, for example, have lost their effectiveness in evangelism through covetousness. The Bible says, "Do not wear yourself out to get rich; have the wisdom to show restraint" (Proverbs 23:4). Other believers are tempted to "water down" the gospel message in order to not offend those to whom they are trying to witness. We need to be cautious in order to not compromise the gospel of our Lord Jesus Christ.

May God grant that we develop in our hearts a holy fear about Hell so that we will snatch our loved ones out of the fire. We should all have unsaved friends. After all, our Lord was called "a friend of sinners" (Luke 7:34). Remember we are to be separated from the unsaved, but not in a hard, cold way. God calls us to a warm, living sacrifice that deals with the lost compassionately, courageously, and cautiously.

Jude says we are to hate the sin, not the sinners. In order to be effective in soul winning, we should cautiously avoid sin like the plague. Consider, for example, the great fear today regarding Acquired Immune Deficiency Syndrome, better known as AIDS. That disease has gripped our society with fear. People are fearful of blood transfusions and even casual contact. Would that we—God's people—fear sin in the same way, as we go about our work and witness. That is what Jude called us to do when he wrote, "Be merciful to those who doubt; snatch others from the fire and to others show mercy, mixed with fear—hating even the clothing stained by corrupted flesh."

Solomon said, "He who wins souls is wise" (Proverbs 11:30). I'm so thankful that Johnny Keeton as a seventeen-year-old, took the time to approach me after a basketball game to tell me about Jesus. He did it compassionately and courageously (and I might add cautiously). He led me to a saving knowledge of Jesus Christ. Somewhere, someone is to be reached for Christ in a way that no one can reach quite as well as you. Perhaps that someone is a sincere doubter who should be approached with compassion. Perhaps that someone is living in open and sinful rebellion, on the very edge of Hell, and should be dealt with courageously and urgently. Or perhaps that person is wallowing in the filth of sin and should be approached with caution. May God grant that as authentic believers we might be educated, insulated, and dedicated to deal with the lost sympathetically. Orthodoxy without compassion is hypocrisy.

CHAPTER EIGHT
Apostasy Viewed Pragmatically

To him who is able to keep you from falling and to present you before his glorious presence without fault and with great joy—to the only God our Savior be glory, majesty, power and authority, through Jesus Christ our Lord, before all ages, now and forevermore! Amen (Jude 24-25).

I. THE SOVEREIGNTY OF GOD
II. THE SECURITY OF THE BELIEVER

Jude wrote much about apostasy in his Epistle. We have studied this "falling away" theoretically, apologetically, synthetically, apathetically, prophetically, cosmetically, and sympathetically. Now we take a look at apostasy from a pragmatic viewpoint. *Webster's New World Dictionary* defines pragmatic as "concerned with actual practice, everyday affairs." How should apostasy affect our everyday attitudes and behavior?

Jude made clear throughout his letter that he was not addressing the possibility of a genuine believer falling from grace. Far from it! In fact, the phrase "falling from grace" is a misnomer. Grace is God's unmerited favor, and we do not fall from grace. We fall into grace! Thus Jude began and ended his Epistle with some of the strongest words in the Bible concerning the true believer's security in Christ.

In most of his letter, Jude addressed his readers in the third person. As he concluded his Epistle he moved to the second person as if to get up close and personal with us in closing.[1] He ends his letter with a note of hope during these dark days of apostasy. His final words are intended to assure us that we can make it! After all has been said and done, we need to remember that our hope is rooted in two important truths: the sovereignty of God and the security of the believer. We find these two truths intertwined in the last two verses of the Epistle of Jude.

I. THE SOVEREIGNTY OF GOD

"Now to Him who is able..." (Jude 24). Jude wanted all of us to know that God is sovereign. It may appear that the spirit of apostasy is winning out, but no! God is omniscient, omnipresent, and omnipotent. He "is able." God's heroics are not confined to bygone days. Jude did not write, "He was able." Nor are we dealing with a God who is powerless today but offers bright hope for tomorrow. Jude did not write, "He shall be able." He wrote "To him who is able." God was able in the past, and He will be able in the future, but the good news is—He is able right now!

We do not often use the word "sovereignty" today. Those influenced by a spirit of apostasy avoid it because they do not want a God who rules over them. The word *sovereignty* speaks of a king who is able to do what he wants to do. Likewise, God does what He pleases and is always pleased with what He does. He is able to do anything.

If your need is grace, "God is able to make all grace abound to you, so that in all things at all times, having all that you need, you will abound in every good work" (2 Corinthians 9:8).

If you need to overcome temptation you can know that "because he himself suffered when he was tempted, he is able to help those who are being tempted" (Hebrews 2:18).

If you need salvation you can be assured that "He is able to save completely those who come to God through him, because he always lives to intercede for them" (Hebrews 7:25).

If you need security, have confidence in knowing "that is why I am suffering as I am. Yet I am not ashamed, because I know whom I have believed and am convinced that he is able to guard what I have entrusted to him for that day" (2 Timothy 1:12).

God is sovereign. He is able! The church today is in danger of being infiltrated and undermined by those who are influenced by the spirit of apostasy. Jude warned us against this danger, and in closing he reminded us that the only source of power for combating apostasy is the sovereignty of God.

Jude carried on the theme of God's sovereignty in verse 25. Our limited human language cannot begin to fully describe the meaning of the four words he used in this verse in his crescendo of a benediction. Who can adequately describe the *glory* of God? Who can even begin to describe the *majesty* of God? What about the *power* of God? Can you describe the *authority* of God? These words remind us that God is sovereign; they speak to us of His omniscience, omnipresence, and omnipotence.

Our God is omniscient. In Jude's words, "To the only wise God" (25, KJV). Although this word, "wise," is omitted in the most ancient manuscripts, it nevertheless is true. Paul concluded his Roman letter with virtually the same words: "to the only wise God be glory forever through Jesus Christ! Amen" (Romans 16:27).

God can give us the wisdom we need. He is able. There are many false teachers who are full of knowledge, but they have no wisdom. God alone is wise. His promise to His people is found in James 1:5: "If any of you lacks wisdom, he should ask God, who gives generously to all without finding fault, and it will be given to him." Jude wrote about God's majesty. He reminds us of the splendor of this King who is over all and knows all. Our God is a sovereign God who is omniscient.

Our God is also omnipresent. In Jude's words, He has "dominion" (25, KJV). He is everywhere present. We are reminded that the psalmist said, "His kingdom rules over all" (Psalm 103:19). "Dominion" speaks of God's strong rule over all the universe. He is everywhere present "now and forevermore." The psalmist wrote:

> Such knowledge is too wonderful for me, too lofty for me to attain. Where can I go from your Spirit? Where can I flee from your presence? If I go up to the heavens, you are there; if I make my bed in the depths, you are there. If I rise on the wings of the dawn, if I settle on the far side of the sea, even there your hand will guide me, your right hand will hold me fast (Psalm 139:6-10).

Our God is omnipotent too. In Jude's words, He has "authority." Some versions use the word "power." There are different Greek words for power. One of them, *dunamis,* is the word used in Romans 1:16: "the gospel...is the power of God for the salvation of everyone who believes." It is the word from which we get the word "dynamite". Another word, *exousia,* means "the right or the authority." This is the word Jude used here. Our God has all authority. Incidentally, it is the same word used in the great commission when Jesus said, "All authority in heaven and on earth has been given to me" (Matthew 28:18).

Jude closed with this impressive reminder of the greatness of God. I believe he was convinced that if we could ever grasp this truth, we would never be deceived or led astray by apostates or other false teachers. When we see this picture of our majestic, powerful, sovereign Lord who sits on Heaven's throne, it puts the audacity of anemic apostasy into proper perspective. Apostasy will be defeated because God is sovereign. He is able!

II. THE SECURITY OF THE BELIEVER

Jude began his Epistle with a message regarding the security of the believer when he reminded us that we are "kept by Jesus Christ" (1). He ended his Epistle in the same way: "To him who is able to keep you from falling" (24). Why? When we read Jude some of us are prone to ask, "Is there any hope? So many fall away. Do we have any hope that we can be secure?" We are like the man to whom Jesus prefaced His healing by saying, "Do you believe that I am able to do this?" (Matthew 9:28)

Jude's words provide the answer—God "is able." He reemphasized that the true believer will make it. His words remind us that we are secure in this life and also in the next life.

Secure in This Life

We live in a world that is uncertain politically, economically, materially, socially, nationally, internationally, and many other ways. But amid this uncertainty, God tells us that we can be secure in this life. In Jude's words, God "is able to keep you from falling" (24). It is wonderful to know that one day God will present us faultless before the throne. How encouraging it is to know too that in the meantime He is able to keep us from falling. We are secure in this life.

It is extremely important to know that we are secure in this life. I recall an unforgettable experience when my family moved to Fort Lauderdale. The hustle and bustle of a metropolitan area with a population of more than one million people was quite different from the quiet, little Oklahoma town we had called home only a few weeks earlier. Our oldest daughter, Wendy, was four years old. Each time we would leave our home and drive in the strange surroundings, facing endless lines of traffic, I remember vividly how obsessed she was with the question, "We will be able to get home, won't we, Daddy?" It is important for children to know that they will be able to get home. It is also important for us, the children of God, to know that we will be able to get home. How important it is to know that we do not have to wonder from day to day whether we are saved or lost. How important it is to know that God will keep us from stumbling. We are secure in this life.

The word "falling" is properly translated "stumbling" in the *New King James Version.* This is an interesting point. Stumbling is the act that precedes falling. God is not simply able to keep us from falling, He is able to keep us from stumbling! If a Christian does stumble, it is not because God has failed him or her. However when we by an act of our will choose to rebel against God and His Word, we not only stumble but virtually fall flat on our faces. As long as we keep ourselves "in God's love" through Bible study, prayer, and holy living, our feet will not stumble. God is able to keep us from stumbling. We are secure in this life.

Secure in the Next Life

Jude wrote, "And to present you before his glorious presence without fault and with great joy" (24). No person is faultless today. We all have spots and wrinkles. But one day we will be like the Lord Jesus. On that day (because of His blood) we will stand before the throne "faultless." The Bible says, "Dear friends, now we are children of God and what we will be has not yet been made known. But we know that when he appears, we shall be like him, for we shall see him as he is" (1 John 3:2). We shall be like Him, and He is without blemish or spot!

How is that going to happen? At the rapture of the church, the Bible says that we will be "changed—in a flash, in the twinkling of an eye" (1 Corinthians 15:51-52). When we are saved, we are immediately justified in the spirit. As we grow in Christ's grace and knowledge, we are progressively sanctified in the soul. And on that grand and glorious day when we are presented faultless, we will ultimately be glorified in the body. We will be presented faultless before the throne. Paul wrote on this subject in his letter to the Ephesians:

> ...Christ loved the church and gave himself up for her to make her holy, cleansing her by the washing with water through the word, and to present her to himself as a radiant church, without stain or wrinkle or any other blemish, but holy and blameless (Ephesians 5:25-27).

It is important to note that both Paul and Jude used the same Greek word, *amomos,* which means "without blemish," to describe our condition when we are presented to the Bridegroom. This same word is used to describe the Lord Jesus in Peter's Epistle:

> For you know that it was not with perishable things such as silver or gold that you were redeemed from the empty way of life handed down to you from your forefathers, but with the precious blood of Christ, a lamb without blemish or defect (1 Peter 1:18-19).

This is what John meant when he said that when Christ appears we will be like him (1 John 3:2).[2] We will be without blemish. Or, as Jude said, He will present us "before his glorious presence without fault and with great joy."

On the lonely island of Patmos John received a glimpse of the day when we will be presented without blemish. He wrote:

> Then I heard what sounded like a great multitude, like the roar of rushing waters and like loud peals of thunder, shouting: "Hallelujah! For our Lord God Almighty reigns. Let us rejoice

and be glad and give him glory! For the wedding of the Lamb
has come, and his bride has made herself ready" (Revelation
19:6-7).

According to John, on that great day the marriage supper of the
Lamb will take place. Jewish weddings during Biblical times throw
considerable light on this feast. First, there was the stage of the
marriage covenant when the groom would leave his father's house
and travel to his prospective bride's home to settle and pay a
ransom price. When the agreement was made the second stage
would begin during which the bride and groom would drink wine
as a symbol of unity. Now they were considered to be married
although they did not begin living together. The third stage began
after the groom had prepared a place for his bride. He would come
back for his bride unannounced. When people in the neighborhood
saw him coming they would shout, "Behold the bridegroom cometh!"
Thus they would forewarn the bride to get ready. In the fourth
stage, the groom would get the bride, take her to his father's house
for the wedding ceremony, and present her before the father.

What an obvious picture this is of that day when our Lord Jesus
will present us faultless before the throne. Just as the Jewish
bridegroom left his father's house and traveled to the home of the
prospective bride to pay the ransom price, so the Lord Jesus
Christ, two thousand years ago, left the glories of Heaven and His
Father's house to enter this sin-cursed earth to pay the price of our
salvation. He purchased us with His own blood at Calvary. Paul
wrote, "You were bought at a price. Therefore honor God with your
body" (1 Corinthians 6:20).

After the marriage agreement was finalized, the Jewish bride
and groom drank wine as a symbol of unity. Likewise the Lord
Jesus Christ, the evening before His crucifixion, took the cup as a
symbol of our unity with Him. Just as the Jewish bridegroom
returned to his father's house to prepare a place for his bride, so
the Lord Jesus Christ before Calvary declared, "I am going there to
prepare a place for you. And if I go and prepare a place for you, I
will come back and take you to be with me that you also may be
where I am (John 14:2b-3).

Next, just as the Jewish bridegroom, after making the prepara-
tions, returned unannounced to receive his bride, so the Lord

Jesus Christ will return unannounced. With a loud shout He will receive His bride—those of us who have been redeemed. Just as people would shout, "Behold the bridegroom cometh," many pastors around the world are sounding the shout loudly and clearly today. As Biblical prophecies are fulfilled and events point to the second coming of Christ, many faithful preachers are shouting at the top of their lungs, "Behold the bridegroom cometh."

Finally, just as the Jewish bridegroom would receive his new bride and take her away to his father's house for the wedding, so the Lord Jesus Christ will come and receive us, taking us away to the great marriage supper of the Lamb. At that time He will present us "without fault and with great joy."

What should be our response as believers? When a bride is about to be married—as we are to Christ—I have noticed that she takes two important courses of action. She accepts the invitation of the bridegroom, otherwise there would be no wedding. She also makes herself as lovely as she can for the ceremony. The question is, have you accepted the invitation of your Bridegroom, the Lord Jesus Christ? If so, are you making yourself as lovely as you can for the marriage supper? Are you keeping yourself in the love of Christ?

Note carefully that the Lord Jesus will present us—His bride—faultless before the Father's throne "with great joy" (Jude 24). Incidentally, Christ's anticipation of this "joy" helped Him to endure the agony of the cross. That is what the Bible means when it says, "Let us fix our eyes on Jesus, the author and perfecter of our faith, who for the joy set before him endured the cross, scorning its shame, and sat down at the right hand of the throne of God" (Hebrews 12:2). The "joy set before him" is that one day He will present us faultless before the presence of His Father.[3] Our Lord Jesus Christ is a faithful and loving Bridegroom.

It is one thing for God to keep us from falling, but quite another to present us "without fault" before the throne. We can never make ourselves faultless, but the Lord Jesus can. He has opened a fountain where we can wash away our sin and become clean. William Cowper wrote:

> There is a fountain filled with blood
> Drawn from Immanuel's veins,

And sinners plunged beneath that flood
Lose all their guilty stains:

Dear dying Lamb, Thy precious blood
Shall never lose its pow'r,
Till all the ransomed Church of God
Be saved to sin no more:

E'er since by faith I saw the stream
Thy flowing wounds supply,
Redeeming love has been my theme
And shall be till I die.

After all is said and done, God is sovereign and we are therefore secure in this life and in the next life—"now and forevermore."

When Jude laid down his pen, all that was left to say was "amen." And we join him in saying "amen" because all has been said. However, there is a real sense in which all has not been done. What is our part? In Jude's words, it is to "contend for the faith that was once for all entrusted to the saints" (3). We do this by loving the faith, learning the faith, living the faith and loosing the faith. As we await His glorious appearing, contending for the faith involves heeding a serious warning from the lips of our Lord to beware of those in sheep's clothing

Notes

Chapter 1
1. Maxwell Coder, *Jude : the Acts of the Apostates* (Chicago: Moody Press, 1958) 8.
2. Samuel Gordon, *Jewels from Jude* (Belfast: Ambassador Productions, 1985) 19.
3. John MacArthur, Jr., *Beware the Pretenders* (Wheaton, IL: Victor, 1980) 17.
4. Coder, *Jude,* 10.
5. C. H. Spurgeon, *The Treasure of the New Testament,* 4 vols. (Grand Rapids: Zondervan, 1950) 4:628.

Chapter 2
1. *Lange's Commentary on the Holy Scriptures,* 12 vols. (Grand Rapids: Zondervan, 1960) 12:13.
2. Gordon, *Jewels from Jude,* 35.
3. *The Pulpit Commentary,* 23 vols. (New York: Funk and Wagnalls, 1950) 22:4.
4. H. A. Ironside, *The Epistles of John and Jude* (Neptune, NJ: Loizeaux, 1931) 15.

Chapter 3
1. MacArthur, *Beware the Pretenders,* 25.
2. Coder, *Jude,* 20.
3. Warren Wiersbe, *Be Alert* (Wheaton, IL: Victor, 1984) 133.
4. Lee Scarborough, *Gospel Messages* (Nashville: Broadman, 1922) 82.
5. William Barclay, *The Letters of John and Jude* (Philadelphia: Westminster, 1958) 212.

Chapter 4
1. MacArthur, *Beware the Pretenders,* 41.
2. Coder, *Jude,* 27.
3. J. N. D. Kelly, *A Commentary on the Epistles of Peter and Jude* (Grand Rapids: Baker, 1969) 258.

4. Barclay, *The Letters of John and Jude,* 216.
5. Gordon, *Jewels from Jude,* 71.

Chapter 5
1. MacArthur, *Beware the Pretenders,* 55.
2. *The Wesleyan Commentary,* 6 vols. (Grand Rapids: Baker, 1977) 6:393.
3. Wiersbe, *Be Alert,* 144.
4. Barclay, *The Letters of John and Jude,* 221.
5. Coder, *Jude,* 73.

Chapter 6
1. *The Century Bible,* 17 vols. (London: Caxton Publishing, 1953) 17:337.
2. Ironside, *Epistles of John and Jude,* 40.
3. Kelly, *Epistles of Peter and Jude,* 272.
4. Coder, *Jude,* 79.
5. Ironside, *Epistles of John and Jude,* 44.

Chapter 7
1. Gordon, *Jewels from Jude,* 160.
2. Coder, *Jude,* 106.
3. MacArthur, *Beware the Pretenders,* 90.
4. Alexander Maclaren, *Expositions of Holy Scripture,* 17 Vols. (Grand Rapids: Baker, 1982) 17:97.
5. H. L. Willmington, *Willmington's Guide to the Bible* (Wheaton, IL: Tyndale House, 1982) 530.
6. Wiersbe, *Be Alert,* 160.
7. *Preacher's Homiletic Commentary,* 31 Vols. (Grand Rapids: Baker, 1980) 30:396.

Chapter 8
1. *Lange's Commentary on the Holy Scriptures,* 12:33.
2. Coder, *Jude,* 124.
3. James Smith and Robert Lee, *Handfuls on Purpose,* 12 vols. (Grand Rapids: Eerdmans, 1947) 12:156.

Select Bibliography

Barclay, William, *The Letters of John and Jude.* Philadelphia: Westminster Press, 1958.

The Century Bible. 17 vols. London: Caxton Publishing Company, 1953.

Coder, Maxwell. *Jude, The Acts of the Apostates.* Chicago: Moody Press, 1958.

Gordon, Samuel. *Jewels From Jude.* Belfast: Ambassador Productions, 1985.

Ironside, H. A. *The Epistles of John and Jude.* Neptune, NJ: Loizeaux Brothers, Inc., 1931.

Kelly, J. N. D. *Epistles of Peter and of Jude.* Peabody MA: Hendrickson Publishers, 1969.

Lange's Commentary on the Holy Scriptures. 12 vols. Grand Rapids: Zondervan Publishing House, 1960.

MacArthur, John, Jr. *Beware the Pretenders.* Wheaton, IL: Victor Books, 1980.

MacLaren, Alexander. *Exposition of Holy Scripture.* 17 vols. Grand Rapids: Baker Book House, 1982.

The Pulpit Commentary. 22 vols. Peabody MA: Hendrickson Publishers, 1984.

Preacher's Homiletic Commentary. 31 vols. Grand Rapids: Baker Book House, 1980.

Robertson, Archibald. *Word Pictures in the New Testament.* 6 vols. Nashville: Broadman Press, 1958.

Scarborough, Lee. *Gospel Messages.* Nashville: Broadman Press, 1922.

Smith, James and Rober Lee, *Handfuls on Purpose.* 5 vols. Grand Rapids: Eerdmans Publishing Company, 1980.

Spurgeon, C. H. *Treasury of the New Testament.* 4 vols. Grand Rapids: Zondervan Publishing Co., 1950.

The Wesleyan Commentary. 6 vols. Grand Rapids: Baker Book House, 1977.

Wiersbe, Warren W. *Be Alert.* Wheaton, IL: Victor Books, 1984.

Willmington, H. L. *Willmington's Guide to the Bible.* Wheaton, IL: Tyndale House, 1981.

Wuest, Kenneth S. *Word Studies in the Greek New Testament.* Grand Rapids: Eerdmans, 1969.